Journey of the Soul

Journey of the Soul

B. LEONILLA AGEIRA

Y. K. PUBLISHERS
**BLOCK 77, SANJAY PLACE
AGRA.**

© **Author**

1999 (First Edition)

ISBN-81-85070-73-3

Published by :
Yogendra Kumar Jain
For **Y. K. Publishers**
Block-77, Sanjay Place.
AGRA-282002 (U.P.) INDIA

Laser Typeset at :
ACE Softwares, F-40/273, Sky Tower, Sanjay Place, Agra.

Printed at :
Rashtra Rachna Printers, Delhi - 110092

To my parents,
Celine and Ligoury Ageira,
my first teachers
during this lifetime.

FOREWORD

After having read the manuscript of the work by Dr. (Ms) B. Leonilla Ageira, and her efforts to reorganize some of the thoughts in the lights of comments made, re-reading the reorganized manuscript was a pleasure.

All those involved in Behavioural Sciences today will admit the great importance of SELF-KNOWLEDGE in all fields of action. This is particularly so when we speak of leadership, when we speak of Happiness, when we speak of Social Work, and even when we speak of God and His love and concern for people, and human relationship with God.

Leonilla's handling the 'Journey of the Soul' from vartious aspect, and particular the aspect of the power and beauty 'within oneself' is interesting and educative, particularly when she handles the ways and means of exploring the 'riches' available within oneself.

Far too many people today tend to make others their 'ideals' to the extent of aping them so much that the potential within themselves is partially or even totally neglected. Leonilla's work in this book will, I am confident, put things in proper perspective and will be an encouragement to one and all is discovering themselves and their potentials to grow a fully human life of happiness and satisfaction: not only for themselves, but also for all those who come in contact with them.

Whether in the area of development of consciousness, transformation of self or significance of meditation in the pursuit of happiness, the author takes genuine pain to place before her readers profound realities in as simple a way as possible. This makes reading easy, and following of the thought process easier.

The material available in this work of Leonilla will be of great use not only to Scholars who wish to make an in-depth study in behavioural sciences, but also to students of management and psychology who are interested in vital area of human relationships.

Rev. Dr. Percival Fernandes Ph. D.
Director
St. John's National Academy of Health Sciences,
Bangalore-560034.

PREFACE

All human beings in this world have a desire to be happy and also a desire to feel powerful within. It is important to believe that this is possible. When we believe that it is possible we give priority to explore the path towards happiness and the power within us. When we believe that it is not possible to find the power and happiness within, we create suffering for ourselves. This suffering is a direct result of our ignorance about who we are and until we become conscious of our innerself we will continue to create suffering for ourselves. When we become conscious of our innerself we will meet God within. God within is the source of all wisdom and power. It is possible to achieve this meeting with God during this lifetime only if one wants it and goes for it.

The present popular perspective of the world in which we live is problem centered. It seeks to explain 'what problems we have, and why we have these problems. This perspective is also competitive. Other people in the neighbourhood and colleagues become the yardsticks to decide on the image and the personality one must have, then this image or personality is projected out to others in order to get acceptance. Unless they think and make a show that they are better than others or richer than others they feel unhappy and become restless. This way of living hardly gives an opportunity to explore the riches within and to be oneself. One can be really happy only by being oneself. Thus people produce the misery of their life. The greater the success in building this image the greater is the shallowness and unhappiness.

LET ME TELL YOU A GREAT SECRET
WHEN YOU LET GO THE IDEA OR IMAGE OF WHO YOU ARE
THE POSSIBILITY OF MEETING THE REAL YOU OPENS UP

Growing through the present perspective of the world we learn what is wrong within us. For example, Christianity can be so obsessed with sin and original sin that often it tends to forget the blessing bestowed by God on the Creation. This tendency is expressed in teaching the young children how they have inherited original sin and how and why human person is ultimately is the root of all evil. There is not sufficient emphasis on graces received from God. We also do not find much being mentioned about an original blessing given by God. If we all are children of God then why would a loving parent make you inherit so much of negativity ? Gods creation is meant to be a blessing. God who is love can only bless you and cannot curse you. It is we who curse ourselves. Hence it is important now to learn to bless ourselves and bless the whole creation. In fact a sufficient emphasis on graces bestowed by God could foster a more optimistic view of life.

The perspective of the world, naturaly helps us to build an image of 'self'. It does not help us to know who we are. However it does push people sometime or other to face questions like 'who am I' ? and what is the purpose of my life ? Isn't it surprising that most of us generally do not even want to face these questions and feel strange about those who ask them. However all of us are unconsciously faced with the two questions: who am I ? and what is the purpose of my life ? Hence there is an urgency to find an alternative perspective of living in order to understand self, others and rest of the creation. This will inturn heal the aspects in present relationships which create stress and build new relationships with self, others, the rest of the creation and God. This book will help you to do that.

The awareness of this search for truth, the search for God is already the result of a long journey the soul has undertaken. Once she/he is aware of this search then another part of the journey beings. The person then seeks consciously until then the search for wholeness within is unconscious one.

APPRECIATIONS

In bringing out this book, I have received support from many. But I will be failing in my duty if I do not express my appreciations to the following individuals.

I want to thank Dr. Varma, former Director of NIMHANS, Bangalore, for encouraging me to complete this work and publish the book.

There is a deep sense of gratitude and appreciation to Rev. Dr. Percival Fermandes, Director of St. John's National Academy of Health Sciences, Bangalore, for his foreword. I appreciate his astute reading of the manuscript amidst his busy schedule and giving his wise and critical comments which helped me to reorganise some of my thoughts and give the book a final shape.

I gratefully acknowledge the support rendered by Mr. Victor Tauro and Fr. Wiliam Martis and I thank Mrs. Uma Maheshwari for her secretarial assistance.

My special thanks to Mr. Y. K. Jain of Y. K. Publishers, Agra.

My appreciations also go to all the participants of my workshops for daring to be open and giving their feedback.

No. 90, 'VIKAS', 8th Block   **B. Leonilla Ageira**

Koramanangala

Bangalore-560 095 (Karnataka)

CONTENTS

1

Journey to the Other Land

I wanted to begin long back but I could not start, today I have discovered my movements, and want to stop what I did not begin.

Some time back, I disappeared in to oblivion, there I found the path. Ah I said, I have been treading this path since years yet have been searching for it. Where does it lead me to ?

I heard a voice whispering softly "this path is your own creation how are you going to direct it hereafter ?

You can leave it unfinished too."

There was — a time I used to allow my restlessness to walk ahead of me. It used to guide me to the path. We used to walk together over time. Time and self share a relationship. Time is immortal, it is there creating a void, a vacuum. It itself is the void. It is constant. A constant path, self is moving, passing with its restlessness in this void. It is people who name this as past, present, and future.

This actually is the past, present and future of animate beings and inanimate objects. People feel secure while they are in touch with the morning, noon and evening. The passing me does not feel morning, noon or evening. I myself have become the time, the void and the path.

When I reached the destination, the restlessness disappeared. Since we have been companions for long I cling to it. Then I made goodbye to this dear companion knowing that I am the path and I am not the same person continuously, every moment I keep on changing, just as no one put their foot twice in the same stream of water.

When I stop filling the void, I meet face to face with the void. The void liberates me. Then I pass through it, being aware of the immortal, naked being that I AM, eternally.

While walking across the path, I experienced the stillness of the new moon, wishing that it should be my permanent abode, I stopped.

And lo a voice whispered, "go on", walk, walk, walk and walk.

Then I saw the grass and tree swaying elegantly to the morning breeze as if welcoming the rising sun. The coolness of the breeze sent shivers down my spine.

I watched the moss covered rocks on the slope of the mountain where I stood and knew that they are alive, the earth and the cosmos are alive too and at that moment I realized stillness and movement co-existed.

Why does a lone bird draw my attention so much. Frances kept on wondering. Today once again there she was grazing at the lake, she was obivious of the fact that she had moved four hours ahead in time.

Unaware of the surroundings and unaware of her own movements, she had been moving in the void. Her whole being was longing to mingle with the calmness of lake. Her craving kept on increasing, as she moved over the constant path called time, to be one with the stillness of water. She still did not know what It was that kept on calling her to lake. Her restlessness increased, could she ever be one with the stillness ?

How futile was her struggle, with a deep sigh, that made her feel the depth of her pain, she turned back to go to her house and at that instant, a lone kite drew her attention. The kite was flying alone. At that instant she understood why a lone bird attracted her. It reminded her of the path. A part of human journey which every human being had to undertake alone. One time or other every human being had to make up her or his mind to be with the void and become the void. Only human beings could do this. No one could accompany or be accompanied for this part of the journey. Every one has to do it alone. After doing this one would get to know the secret of who one is.

Frances remembered Sigmund Freud's (1938) statement, "the moment a man questions the meaning and value of life, he is sick, since objectively neither has any existence, by asking this question one is merely admitting to a store of unsatisfied libido to which something close must have happened, a kind of fermentation leading to sadness and depression. I am afraid these explanations of mine are not very wonderful. Perhaps because I am too pessimistic."For Frances if one did not make an attempt to know the meaning and purpose of life at some point of time or other the person merely existed like creature other than human being, without finding and relishing the great treasures of life.

It is but natural for a living system to strive for homeostasis. One has to undergo a process, which gives one a mixture of pain, frustration and joy. It is good to be sensitive and feel these feelings immensely. This is how one develops and grows. A caterpillar undergoes metamorphosis to become a butterfly and fly into the freedom, that is in store. Each one of us have to grow and liberate oneself and be the real self that each one is.

It is wonderful experience to be liberated and to be oneself. Probity to self is virtue and the readiness to jump into the darkness, into the cloud of unknowing is of paramount importance. It is an adventurous task.

It is not the end it is only a beginning of living. One must choose to make this adventurous journey itself joyous.

If one waits for the end to be happy while striving to reach the goal one can be happy few times in life. But if you make the journey itself joyous you can always be happy.

The secret of life is discovered not when life is devoid of obstacles but when it is rough and tumble.

Uncertainty is a pathway towards certainty.

Frances sat down on the stone again. She had forgotten that she was treading the constant path time. Once again she started moving in the vacuum. Her gaze kept on circling around the lake. She let out a half cry of pain and joy when there was a sudden realization that the kite was alive. The kite was on its own. It had chosen to fly around the lake. She had almost forgotten to breathe when she experienced a mixture of vehement of astonishment and perplexity, the moment she was aware that the kite was there with a purpose.

Now the simple fact was clear. Slightly away from her seat a carcass was lying. There was no one to own it. It was inactive, without any awareness of its existence. The kite had detected it and was crackling to own it.

The kite was aware that the carcass was there and it needed it, so that it may continue to exist.

France now turned here attention to lake. It was there existing as still as before. The current beneath the surface was not visbble. As she moved forward in time, gradually light started fading. In the absence of light, darkness had upper hand. Hence darkness started covering her, the lake and the surroundings. It was a homely environment. the familiar silent darkness of the lake sent chills down her spine. It was horribly good and exciting. Once again she had the uncomfortable craving to blend herself with the stillness and silence, as a drop of water would mingle in the wine. Slowly and gradually she faded in the obivion to the world and got in touch with the reality.

She was lying in the darkness, waiting for the faint light to appear. She did not want to fumble in the darkness. Darkness was good when one wanted to be still, inhaling the cold breeze that pierced once Soul.

She started gaining momentum as radiant glow met her wondering misty eyes. The mist dissappeared as she kept on experiencing the soft comforting warmth of the morning sun. She moaned with joy. Once again she was awake and she could be her own. It was a joyous walk, learning to be and live alone for the part of the journey. It was a painful happiness to fall and get up on ones own. there was so much to learn in this strange world covered with beautiful sunshine.

Surely a strange world indeed. A world where people live by forming what is called a society. An individual living at a given point of time, in a particular society had to allow herself/himself to be carried by the tide. If she/he dared to swim against the tide then she/he would be ostracized by the society. This organism that is society, had its own self, hence human beings who are units forming the organism, believed that can not have the individual self. Hence these units inculcated the rational and irrational beliefs of the organism and believed they were living according to the norms of the society. The units feared to stand alone, since the time they were born they were taught that they are only a part of the organism and were not whole as an individual. As a result of this teaching the tremendous potential within each unit remained dormant. They did not want to develop their potential. They feared growth and escaped from freedom. only a very few were courageous enough to search and discover their individual self. They discovered the secret that a human being is a microcosm. Everything that was in the Macrocosm was also there in the microcosm. By going through and inward journey one could discover and know the microcosm and by doing this you could know the

Macrocosm as well. The microcosm has a great storage of energy and power. It was as powerful as the Macrocosm. Hence human beings were 'part' of the Macrocosm as well as the 'whole'. IN FACT THE PART COULD NOT AND NEVER EXISTED SEPARATELY FROM THE WHOLE. One could not discover the secret and also retain their micro identity. Those who discovered this secret were fortunate and experienced the wholeness within. Thus were fortunate to experience the wholeness within.

Now the light was evenly spread. Frances stretched her limbs and got up. There was freshness all around.

"Fances" all of a sudden a familiar voice called out her name. It was her mother asking her to join the morning prayer.

Frances had decided to choose and to live. She did not want to be pushed by the tide. She was ready to fall and experience the pain that would comfort her. That is why she thought a long walk on the uphill is better than the morning prayer. She wore her trecking suit and started walking.

2

Development of Consciousness

'Actually you could creatively come out with a great plan and blow the world around you.' Frances told Maryann.

'It sounds too fantastic about me, I am getting scared.' Maryann said.

'Why do you get scared if it sounds fantastic about you Maryann ?'

'You know I have a certain background so I may be having problems...' .

Isn't this true for many of us when someone tells us we have problems we believe it easily whereas if someone says we are fantastic we have a difficulty to believe it. We are scared to believe it. why ?

We are scared to believe that we are capable of fantastic. Simultaneously we long for the fantastic but we settle down to believing, 'we have problems, something is wrong with us and we are incapable of achieving anything higher,' We take the beaten path, and comfortably believe that we are weak.

ACTUALLY WE ARE NEITHER WEAK NOR STRONG
WE JUST ARE.

We also find plenty of excuses and justify why we cannot achieve what we want. This negativity about ourselves, others, the world and even God has become a part of us. Intuitively we know we are powerful and we are scared of this power we own. We often disown the power and choose negativity. Why ?

Negativity is the familiar track, that we are used to tread. It allows us to escape. We are scared of the unfamiliar and the unknown. Generally we feel we are acceptable among our friends and in society when we move on the familiar known track. We are also afraid to be alone.

IMAGINE WHAT KIND OF FAMILY AND FRIENDSHIP WE HAVE CULTIVATED AND WHAT KIND OF REALITY WE HAVE CREATED FOR OURSELVES. THE WORLD THAT WE HAVE BUILT AROUND US HELPS US TO CHOOSE NEGATIVITY SO THAT WE ARE SAFE ON THE FAMILIAR KNOWN TRACK. IT KEEPS US SAFE FROM EXERCISING THE POWER THAT WE POSSESS AND OWNING RESPONSIBILITY FOR OUR ACTION.

When we accept we are powerful then we are spotted and we are going to be in the limelight. This means we have to perform and be responsible for our action. So lurking behind all this is the fear of being responsible for ones action. In the bible we see Adam getting rid of this fear by blaming Eve and holding her responsible for the apple eaten by him, when he was questioned by God for breaking the established norm in garden of Eden. If you walk on your own path then you have to take responsibility for it. If you go according to what is prescribed then you can always blame family, friends and even the whole society for whatever goes wrong and feel safe within. But why are we afraid that things would go wrong if we listen to the voice within the self ? Why do we get conditioned not to have confidence in 'self'.

Once there were two young ladies who were being forced to do nude worship in Goddess Yellamma's temple. After the worship they would be sold to the man who bid the highest money. With great difficulty a group of social workers rescued them from efficient nexus. There was a lot of pressure from the parents to return their daughters. The social workers did not heed to the pressure. Girls said they were convinced they did not want to end up being prostitutes. They wanted to choose a different life for themselves. However when the time came for their departure from the village they wanted to say 'good bye' to their parents. Girls knew it very well once they meet their parents they would not let them go inspite of that they went to meet their parents and never returned.

The dream of liberation from the traditions that oppressed their life was too fantastic for them. They wanted and dreamt about it and even attempted to realise but they did not believe that it was possible to realise it. The conditioning got on their way.

If you dare to dream the dream of your life and again dare enough to make it real then you and you alone are responsible for your action and for your life. If you do not dream your own dreams then all you have is only the junk that is thrown at you by others. Now you choose what you want.

USE ME

Recently I was involved in a discussion with a group of people. People vehemently argued 'how important it was to distrust others. If you are smart then you would not trust anybody. Only the naive, ignorant and stupid people trust others.' One of the beliefs in this group was that 'distrust is important for the survival of self'.

During the earlier part of human history human beings had to struggle with so many odds for survival. During this struggle for survival we have learnt to distrust and to attack others in order to protect ourselves. Distrusting, attacking, controlling, and hoarding are some of the learnt survival mechanisms. This is a particular transitory stage in our growth. We are not meant to stop growing at this stage because the survival techniques themselves are not the desired end products. Even survival itself is not the ultimate purpose of our life. Now most of us seem to mistake the means for goals.

> WE LIKE TO CLING TO OUR SURVIVAL TECHNIQUES
> AS IF THEY ARE THE GOALS OF OUR LIFE
> BECAUSE WE ARE AFRAID OF DEATH.
> BUT THIS CLINGING MERELY GIVES US
> A LONG INSECURE SURVIVAL.
> IT DOES NOT GIVE US A LONG LIFE.
> THE CONSEQUENCE IS LACK OF GROWTH.

We must move forward. Moving forward would mean getting to know the purpose of life and taking steps to move in this direction. But as long as we cling to our old survival techniques we will not know the purpose of life. If you want to know the purpose of your life first you must know yourself. Initially it may seem like jumping in to the unknown darkness but it is a worthwhile exercise. Knowing yourself and knowing the purpose of your life is not a small achievement. In order to achieve this great goal you must start with small steps of becoming familiar with yourself and your inner landscape.

THE EVOLUTION OF THE EGO

The socio-economic structures of society reflect upon the consciousness of an individual and collective consciousness of the members of society.

A newly born child does not distinguish her/himself from the environment and she/he is not conscious of her/himself as a separate being from rest of the world.

The 'ego' is a congnitive structure. Its origins occur in early childhood as a result of interaction between the child and the world. As the infant grows and interacts with the environment, she/he learns to distinguish between 'I' or 'me' and 'you' or 'others'. She/He gradually starts experiencing self in an unique way and differentiates self from others and the rest of the environment. This is how the ego develops. Her/His interactions with significant others and her/his own nature gradually develop into certain patterns helping her to perceive self as a separate individual with unique characteristics. Thus the ego emerges within the frame-work of social interaction.

The basic functions of the ego are similar to that of a chief executive of an organization. The chief executive of an organization acts on behalf of the organisation. She/he assesses the needs, takes care of the needs and executes action for the development of the organization. Similarly the 'ego' essentially develops to take care of the being.

As the ego develops it becomes the reference point around which the person's experiences and coping patterns are organized. Then the person starts deciding and choosing to respond in a certain way in any situation. The individual perceives what she wants as indicated by such statements as "I want", "I know" and "I will". Actually these are the desires of the ego. In fact during these initial stages of consciousness a person mistakes the 'ego' as the 'self'. The ego acts on behalf of the person. Gradually as the child grows into adulthood she/he learns to initiate actions on behalf of self and learns the complex skills of survival as well as how to get what one wants. In this process the 'ego' becomes stronger and stronger.

The reactions of an individual to the environment depend on the person's perception and experience of it. That is why the network of relationships into which one is born and brought up are very important in the growth and development of the ego of a person. The ego itself is the person until the person gets enlightened that she/he is not the ego. Generally most of the interactions between human beings are in fact the interactions between the egos'.

The present mode of living of most of the population is competitive. Competition rather than cooperation is the rule of the game. Cooperation exists mostly when there is self gain. Relationships are also based on what one gets from the other. Love and happiness are also searched outside of oneself. People fall in love in order to get love, to feel loved and to be loved. Actually genuine love wishes the good of the other. She/he is able to be happy with other without having the hidden agenda of service to oneself. Where as an individual living in our society often gets a message that she/he somehow should be better than the other. So people keep on entering into a competitive life style created and maintained in our society by people who are trying to prove that they are better and more successful than the other. A child gradually imbibes this way of living and grows into adulthood.

The subjectively apprehended world is known as the phenomenal field; it represents the totality of experiences of which an individual is aware at the time of action. In fact the phenomenal field determines all behaviour. Generally human beings do not interact with the objective world rather we interact with the subjectively perceived world hence the perception of reality of each individual is different from the other. That is why same person, events and situations give different meaning to different people. Actually it is the individual who perceives or interacts in one way or the other gives meaning to it. Thus the perceived reality is coloured by self. One who sees it makes it beautiful or ugly; full of hope or hopeless.

The phenomenal world constitutes the individual's frame of reference or the congnitive map. Hence the 'cognitive-map' provides coloured glasses to the individual. When you change the colour of the glasses the world looks different.

Gradually a person starts developing more or less stable concept about self. The self-concept is the stable, enduring and more or less permanent aspect of the phenomenal field. The self-concept is also developed by the individual herself/himself. There is not anyone else other than the individual self who is responsible for developing it.

The individual internalises the concepts of good or bad; right or wrong. Behaviour is learnt and the internalisation is done through trial and error methods depending on how efficient a behaviour is to take care of the specific needs of the person. The internalisation is based on one's own judgments with regard to what is appreciated and accepted or rejected punished by the society or insights in terms of what one wants. In other words the person gets conditioned.

The initial stage of the development of consciousness about self as a separate individual is important for the person. The conditioning occurs during this stage. The conditioning occurs in order to take care of the being. Simultaneously it also limits the person from seeing the whole situation. As a consequence of this the person becomes less effective and efficient in developing strategies and implementing action to manage particular situation. In other words it means that the person blocks ones creative energy. During this stage each internalized belief and the behaviour associated with it may act as if they have separate existence and each of these become part of the ego. A person must go through a stage of processing the inner data and dynamics in order to perceive the connection between the beliefs one possesses and the action one executes to deal with a situation.

The degree of integration among the different beliefs varies from individual to individual. Hence a single individual may have conflict within herself/himself, between these different parts of the person. In other words there may be conflict between the different energy parts of the person, specially when the idea or belief in one energy part contradicts with the other.

It is necessary to understand that our thoughts are energies. Hence there is also energy associated with beliefs and ideas. The energy associated with a single belief or idea, may vary in different people since the same idea or belief may mean different to different people. Hence during this stage of internalisation of ideas and behaviour and development of ego, a person might develop intrapsychic conflicts and may lack clarity with regard to what one wants. There may also be imbalance which may become evident in lopsided growth. There are possibilities of a person behaving in an extreme manner in certain aspects. The imbalance persists till the person develops self awareness about oneself.

The socio-economic structures, cultural practices, political situation, all these including the gender, caste and class of the person have an impact on the way the person perceives, experiences and internalises the reality and then forms one's own frame of reference with regard to how she/he wants to be.

Consciously or unconsciously one judges how one should be in order to survive, to be secure, to get: attention, acceptance or love; or to get what one wants in a given society or a culture. A person starts formulating goals and builds strategies to achieve them.

The self-concept of a person includes the following aspects:

(a) how a person perceives oneself: this includes the data collected about oneself by making use of the senses based on actions, thoughts, feelings and the desires of the self and the response of others while interacting with them.

(b) what one thinks of oneself: this depends on what one perceives of oneself, but it need not include everything a person perceives. Many times we disown certain aspects of ourself which are unacceptable or unpleasant to us. This forms the picture the person has of herself. It is also a current view of her appearance, goals, attitudes, background and ability. This also includes gender, the cultural group to which one belongs to, position and status in society.

(c) what one values in oneself: this includes what she/he considers as worthwhile and likes in oneself. The contemporary thought has a lot of influence on this aspect of the self. What is valued in the family and society at large, what is considered as modern and progressive influence the persons thoughts. For example in a materialistic society, making money and other wealth and hoarding these get the priority in a person's life. One who does not have money may start building a low opinion about oneself. This opinion will last until the person becomes aware of oneself and ones consciousness.

(d) how one attempts through various actions to enhance or defend oneself. A person may or may not have a cognitive understanding of this behaviour. It might have unconsciously become a pattern of behaviour in order to protect oneself and to fulfill one's desires. One must realise that ultimately self love is at the core of all these behaviours. Hence thoughts and behaviours are directed towards self preservation or to get the desired object. Feelings are indicators about what the person is feeling about self. Whether the person is feeling secure and moving towards the desired object or is feeling threatened and moving away form the desired object.

Self is the differentiated portion of the phenomenal field which emerges as a result of evaluational interaction with others. It includes the physical self, evaluations of self and definitions of self, that is the self-concept. When an individual conceives of the self as real self, it refers to the way she/he behaves, thinks and feels in real life; or as social self, which refers to the self as perceived by others; and ideal self, which refers to the self that she/he aspires to become.

Developing self awareness is crucial if one wants to improve ones quality of life, to develop better coping mechanisms, to get in touch with ones higher self, to be happy, to get rid of the addictions in the self or to fulfill the need for transformation of self.

One of the ways of engaging in the process of self-awareness is to reflect on these three dimensions of self.

REAL SELF

How I think and behave in real life

How I feel about myself

How I enhance and defend myself

SOCIAL SELF

Self as experienced by others

How do I make contact with others

How do I reach out to others

How much I reveal myself to others

How open I am to the responses of others to me

How I evaluate and respond to the reactions of others

IDEAL SELF

What I would like to be as a person

What I want to feel and do

The closer the three dimensions, the more integrated the person is, the more in touch with her/his humanity.

Self awareness is essential in order to achieve integration of different dimensions of self. Similarly it is also essential to achieve synthesis of various aspects of self, i.e. different internalised ideas, beliefs and the behaviour associated with it. The synthesis and integration help the person to move from imbalance to balance.

Synthesis, integration and balance give more life to the individual. There is healing energy associated with it.

Self cannot be considered as completely formed; it is continuously in a process of 'becoming' through the process of interpersonal and intrapersonal relationships. The self as it finally evolves is a composite of thoughts and feelings which constitutes a person's awareness of her/his individual existence, her/his perception of what she/he has, her/his conception of who she/he is and her/his feelings become the nucleus on which, and in which, and around which experiences are integrated into the uniqueness of the individual.

Soul awareness is one of the crucial aspects in the evolution of a human being. It provides the inner unchanging aspect of self, whereas the body, ego, thoughts and feelings provide the changing aspects.

Carl Rogers and his students developed a scheme of the fully functioning person, a scheme generally referred to as 'self theory', which has been a great help in understanding self. Rogers summarizes this theory in the outline below:

A. The individual has an inherent tendency toward actualizing his organism.

B. The individual has the capacity and tendency to symbolize experiences accurately in awareness.

1. A corollary statement is that he has the capacity and tendency to keep this self-concept congruent with his experience.

C. The individual has a need for positive regard.

D. The individual has a positive self-regard.

E. Tendencies A and B are most fully realized when needs C and D are met. More specifically, tendencies A and B tend to be most fully realized when

1. The individual experiences unconditional positive regard from significant others.

2. The pervasiveness of this unconditional positive regard is made evident through relationships marked by a complete and communicated empathetic understanding of the individual's frame of reference.

F. If the conditions under E are met to a maximum degree, the individual who experiences these conditions will be a fully functioning person.

The increased understanding of self acts as a crucial factor in achieving personal happiness and effective behaviour.

The 'self theory' advocates that, 'A person lives essentially in his or her own personal and subjective world and the self is the central figure in every act.' We relate to everything and to everyone in connection with self. Human beings, animate and inanimate world without any exception we relate consciously or unconsciously with the self and then get meaning and give meaning to it.

Every individual has an inherent tendency towards actualizing the being. It means that the formation of self is accompanied by the unfolding of the person. When this unfolding is not allowed either because of dominant parents or other significant persons or factors, then the person learns to be submissive temporarily. This seems to be the efficient and effective behaviour for the survival of the person. When the situation changes either because of the change within the person or due to external factors then the person may exhibit different behaviour. This way human beings continuously keep on changing themselves. In this process,

'ACTUALLY WE BECOME THE PATH
WHICH ULTIMATELY TAKES US TO WHO WE ARE.'

Human beings have the capacity and tendency to symbolise or organise experiences accurately in awareness in some relationship to self. Symbolization means admitting the experience in a verbal or non-verbal way. When there is incongruence between self and experience , then the person is unable to symbolise or unable to become consciously aware of this experience. It means that the person screens out the experience through defence mechanisms and gets a distorted perception. The experience may also be ignored because there is no perceived relationship to the self structure. That is, a person has the capacity and tendency to keep her/his self-concept congruent with her/his experience.

Every individual has a need for positive regard. Unconditional positive regard is essential in the unfolding of the person and development of self. Then the person becomes more open to experience. Unconditional positive regard makes the person experience the joy of being. It is essential to experience unconditional positive regard not only from significant others but also from oneself.

The pervasiveness of this unconditional positive regard is made evident through relationships marked by a complete and communicated empathetic understanding of the individual's frame of reference. If these conditions are met to a maximum degree, then she/he becomes a fully functioning person. Through unconditional positive regard a person gets a message that she/he as a person is important than anything else. It gives a person confidence to have higher aspirations, to be fearless and go for what one wants. Experiences communicating lack of unconditional positive regard may give to a person the message that objects, events and achievements are more important than the person.

When a person starts believing this then she/he may not feel confident about oneself. The person may still try to achieve in order to get acceptance. Lack of achievement may fill the person with fear of non-acceptance. Hence the person may experience life as torturous and may feel unhappy within. The person may also experience rejection from and resentment towards the significant others.

Since a person's view of self and world determine her feeling and behaviour, so a positive self-concept is a crucial determinant for a person to be healthy and life giving.

The insights on the development of self affirm that,

LOVE IS AT THE CENTER OF ALL PROCESSES
THAT SHAPE THE EMERGENCE OF A FULLY FUNCTIONING
HUMAN BEING.

Hence it may be necessary here to know what love is, since love is understood differently by different people. In my understanding there are three different aspects of genuine love. They are:

(a) wishing genuinely the good of the other,

(b) respecting the free will of the other, and

(c) being able to be happy with the other without desiring or expecting any benefits for self from the other.

Human beings are also interdependent on one another. Self doesn't grow in isolation. An individual forms views, attitudes, opinions regarding oneself which are derived from one's interaction with significant others.

THE SELF-IMAGE

Self-image reflects the concretised and crystallised concept which the individual has formulated by reflecting upon oneself. It reflects a persons opinion about self. For example the juvenile delinquent has a low opinion of self and others; hence she/he degrades herself/himself and others through her/his behaviour. Thus the self-image, that is what a person admits the self to be, acts like a self-fulfilling prophecy. Sometimes people have unrealistic and inflated images about themselves. For example, a middle aged woman may see herself as a slender young girl in the mirror.

Another example is that of a person who thinks oneself as the saviour of the world and in her/his need to be a saint, may idealise herself/himself falsely; since she/he can never attain that fantasised self she/he is instantly exposed to a sense of failure and inadequacy. She/He may either constantly experience herself/himself as a failure since the reality does not match her/his ideal, or in his arrogance of not wanting to accept reality, may retreat into fantasy where she/he can see himself as she/he would like to be. In any case, she/he would be extremely sensitive to criticism and the reality is too painful for her/him. Such a person will have difficulty in interpersonal relationships and thereby foster a sense of isolation and distress.

'Reflected appraisals' of a person's experience contribute to the formation of the self-image. In fact Harry Stack Sylvan (1953) stressed the importance of "reflected appraisals" in creating one's self-image. During the growth of the child, the child is flooded with a number of interpersonal relationships which bring positive or negative attitudes towards herself as she assimilates the views of significant others.

There is a direct relationship between self-concept and the attitude of others, since the formation of self- concept is based on the actual response and perceived response of others towards self. Self-concept can be defined as the opinion one forms about oneself based on one's self reflection. This in turn is based on the feed back one receives from others about oneself and ones own perceptions about self. Self-image is the concretised symbolic representation of the self-concept.

Community is the context in which people are formed. It is the human encounter, the existential meeting of two persons in meaningful relationship, which is the spark igniting the enormous potential of human energy and creativity. It also simultaneously has the potential to mould someone into a dysfunctional unit when the feedback a person receives is based on dysfunctional norms and values. Then the meaning-system based on which one organises oneself itself blocks the growth of the person from becoming into a loving person, though it gives meaning to the person in the particular social context. For example:

(i) In a casteist society a 'Savarna', a person from upper caste, gets a constant feedback of being superior to 'Avarna' by virtue of belonging to a particular caste and vice versa.

(ii) In a patriarchal society like ours men constantly get the feedback that they are superior to women. Women get the feedback that they are nothing in comparison to men and they must obey men.

Though the formation of self-image is an unconscious process it is critically important for a person to be aware of her/his self-image. The self-image of a person keeps on changing depending on the growth of the individual. By being aware a person can alter her/his self-image. Thus one can create the self-image that one wants to have and eliminate the aspects of the self-image that makes a person dysfunctional or does not bring out the best.

When the person moves in the direction of knowing who she/he is and becomes more self aware the image disappears and the person can know herself/himself as she/he is.

SELF-ESTEEM

The figure demonstrates how various aspects contribute in the development of self-esteem.

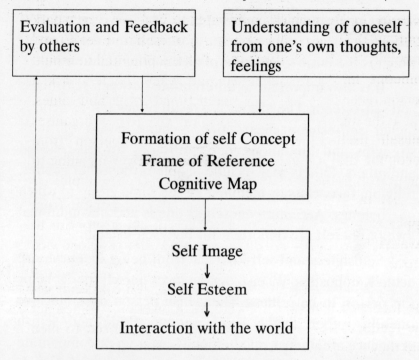

Self-esteem is the dynamic aspect of self-image. Self-esteem crystallise through regularised and recurrent responses of others and when one is consistently treated in the same manner, one's evaluations of oneself are reinforced. If a person has a positive self-image, then she also has a high self-esteem and vice versa. The self-esteem of a person becomes visible in the way she/he treats herself/himself, and interacts with others. Self-esteem is a part of the present consciousness of the person and it determines her/his behaviour.

Unconditional love has a positive impact on the self-esteem. It makes a person feel good about one's existence without asking one to prove oneself. It gives the person an experience, both emtionally and cognitively, of acceptance, whoever and whatever she/he may be. It is not only important to receive unconditional love from others but also from oneself in order to be gentle towards and respect oneself which contributes to one's own growth and unfolding. It also conveys trust in oneself and the Creator, which is the basic foundation of all enabling relationships.

It is also important to differentiate between selfishness and self-esteem. The former is a result of law self-esteem. A higher self-esteem means one is more aware of one's strengths and limitations, one's attitudes towards oneself and others. Others may include people of the other gender, religion, race, class or members of the same group to which one belongs. Accepting oneself as one is and unconditional love of oneself are important for high self-esteem.

Selfishness and self-love, far from being identical, are actually opposites. When a person loves herself then it helps the person to be selfless. The selfish person does not love oneself; rather she/he hates oneself. Pride and selfish arrogance are, in fact, an attempt to cover up or compensate for self-hate. It only indicates that the person's basic beliefs about oneself are negative and that she/he has low self-esteem. If a person views and experiences her/his core as basically good, lovable, satisfied and useful, then her/his life becomes constructive, meaningful and productive.

Maslow, for example, suggests that finding out what a person is really like 'inside, deep down,' is the key to creating a successful personality.

High self-esteem is necessary if one is to trust oneself sufficiently to rely upon it as locus of evaluation, and to search for one's true nature in order to become the self one is called to be. A fully human person is one who trusts herself enough to carry forward her/his deepest inner hopes and most daring visions through which she/he strives to reach her/his highest potential.

POWER RELATIONS

EVERY HUMAN BEING WANTS TO FEEL POWERFUL
AND TO BE IN CONTROL OF THE SITUATION IN WHICH
SHE/HE EXISTS.

There is nothing wrong in this basic desire. The moment we discover who we are this need disappears. Then we will know that there is only one reality. Right now we are in an illusion of being separate from other human beings and other life. Hence there is a tendency to use others and rest of the creation for the benefit of the self. When we discover who we really are then there will not be a choice other than loving others as we love ourselves. We will also then realise that loving others also means loving oneself. Hence LOVE IS AT THE CENTER OF ALL ACTIONS. LOVE IS POWER.

For the time being it is necessary to aware of the need to feel powerful by controlling others and other creation. One should be aware of the kind of 'control' needs one has. Actually no one can control anybody. Life can not be controlled.

LIFE CAN ONLY BE GIVEN
AND ENHANCED

Hence the sense of controlling the 'other' is an illusion.

When the self-esteem of a person is low then the person may adapt methods of controlling others by finding their weakness or by attempting to put others down or by using coercive methods. One may internalise different methods of controlling the other, depending on what is suitable for the person.

THE WHOLE WORLD IS A SCHOOL WHERE
ALL OF US LEARN THE LESSONS THAT WE NEED TO LEARN.

When the self-esteem is low there may also be a tendency in the person to feel insecure, when others become functional. This behaviour also is not all life enhancing. It only increases negativity and negative energy around the person. By being aware one could reduce the negative energy and increase the life enhancing energy. That is why

AWARENESS OF SELF IS HEALING TO THE WORLD.

Socialization is a life long process by which a person develops beliefs, values, attitudes, knowledge, awareness of social expectations and appropriate norms of behaviour. People become socialised to their immediate environment as well as to the larger social context. In this context it is necessary to understand various forces in society which guide the formation and understanding of self, leading to the choice of a certain kind of behaviour and mode of living.

There is a definite relationship between the individual and the social structure. This is because there is a certain thought i.e., a body of beliefs and ideas behind the emergence of a particular kind of social structure, similarly the thought guides the formation of the ego. The ego is formed through the persons interactions with the environment. The person internalises the beliefs or ideas by internalising the prevalent myths, symbols and language and forms ones own perspective of life. The person in this way acquires consciousness. That is why the average individual has acquired consciousness. The conciousness of the group in which one is grown and the consciousness of the society at large shapes the consciousness of the individual. In this way mostly majority of the people's thought, feelings and actions are determined by the contemporary society. This also means that what a person eats, wears and what kind of house one wants to live in, are determined by the society. Even the way one carries one's body is determined by one's thought. A person's thought influences even her/his psycho-physical health and appearance.

HUMAN BEINGS ARE BUNDLES OF BELIEFS
AND BUNDLES OF MEMORIES

The revolution of mind-body medicine was based on a simple discovery that wherever there is a thought there is also a chemical. This insight is a powerful tool to understand why widows are twice likely to develop breast cancer or chronically depressed are four times more likely to get sick. Distressed mental states get converted into the biochemicals that create disease.

The formation of ego takes place in a complex web of relationships. The new generation receives the cultural heritage through socialization, thus the existing social structures and cultural patterns are reproduced and continuity is assured. That is why also change is slow and when there is change, the individuals involved as well as the system and the structure in which the change is introduced experience stress and strain. However once the new behaviour required to deal with the change is successfully learnt the harmony is attained in the system. Hence it is important not to run away from stress and strain.

STRESS AND STRAIN ARE INVITATIONS
TO GROWTH HENCE THEY ARE BLESSINGS THAT HELP US
TO UNEARTH OUR STRENGTH.

Certain aspects of the existing society are both exploitative and oppressive. The oppressive and exploitative aspects of power relations are also reproduced.

IF YOU WANT TRANSFORMED NEW GENERATION THEN
THERE SHOULD BE TRANSFORMATION IN THE PRESENT
GENERATION, AMONG PEOPLE AS WELL AS SOCIO-
ECONOMIC STRUCTURES AND POLITICO-CULTURAL
CONSCIOUSNESS. YOU CAN PASS ON TO THE NEW
GENERATION ONLY WHAT YOU HAVE AT PRESENT
WITH YOU.

Social reality is made up of the constraints of the material world as well as the complex dynamics of various forms of power and privileges that work together in a mutually reinforced process. The dominant groups control the reinforcement process and the outcome of the dynamics.

In the present socio-economic and political context, one of the very basic factors which shapes the formation of the ego is POWER. Power can be understood as the capacity to be in charge of any situation without being disturbed about it, to be aware of this capacity within oneself and to feel comfortable with it. When people are not aware of this capacity within themselves then they do not feel confident about themselves to deal with the situations in which they find themselves. This in turn generates fear. The degree of awareness of this capacity to deal with any situation without allowing the situation to be in charge of them varies from one individual to another.

The journey from dependence to independence also consists in the acquisition of power, which is manifested by possession of material goods and attempts to gain control over others and over the environment. The patterns of being submissive or dominant are manifested in the social relations with members of the group to which one belongs, with or 'other groups. The 'other groups' could be people of the other gender, caste, class and race. To be submissive, or dominating over people of another caste, class or gender, to discriminating against people of other religions, language or race, are all games of control and power over the other.

Living through this process of acquiring power one can often discover that power can not be acquired. If one attempts to know oneself with an uncompromising honesty with oneself one can see through these games. After all where is the limit ? How much of wealth one has to hoard and how much control one has to exercise on others in order to feel powerful ? The tendencies to hoard more than one requires and to exercise control over others mostly is the result of experiencing self in competition with rest of the creation for survival. Hence a need to be in control of the situation is generated.

THE MOMENT WE ARE BORN WE ARE INTRODUCED TO THE ILLUSTION OF SEPARATE EXISTENCE.

So we perceive the 'self' as the center of everything and self preservation determine majority of our actions until we discover that the 'self' does not have independent existence and all life is connected. The inward journey of knowing who we are can free us from the illusion of separate existence.

It is worth mentioning that social reality with its socio-economic structures, cultural patterns, political atmosphere together with its oppressive and exploitative aspects is also reproduced in the institutionalized religions. Because it is controlled and directed by human beings who have acquired consciousness from the contemporary society.

When there are beings with raised awareness interacting with institutions or directing institutions to achieve growth in order to support growth and life, then the impact of the raised consciousness is felt in large groups. This creates more energy that gives life to the universe. This in turn effects and helps in the evolution of consciousness of a large human community. This in turn helps a large number of human beings to evolve their consciousness.

The indicator for evolved consciousness can be understood as people, institutions, community or a society acquiring capacity to make decisions or establish norms in support of having and giving more life to themselves and others.

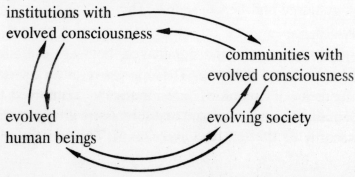

institutions with evolved consciousness

communities with evolved consciousness

evolved human beings

evolving society

For example in the institutional Catholic Church also the gender relations often can be quite oppressive. Until recently woman had to cover their heads in the Church, they could not go to the altar and even now women are barred from being priests. These norms of gender relations historically have emerged based on certain body of beliefs about women. In the recent times accompanied with the change of beliefs there is a change in the position of women in the Church. There is also a change in the norms of man-woman interactions within the Church. There is also an attempt to include women in making decisions which effect their life. These changes definitely indicate growth among men and women who are instrumental to bring about these changes. It also helps other men and women participating in the life of the Church to move in the direction of growth. There can be further transformation in gender relations when more men and women with greater self awareness emerge within the Church and start interacting with the established norms of the Church.

What we see is the social reality which has been created by us is in favour of the dominant groups. This is because the dominant groups are the trend setters of any society. POWER AND CONTROL play a dominant role in designing various relations between groups. These power games are directed towards 'self-gain'. They are self-centered and hence, selfish. There is nothing religious about it.

Submissiveness and dominance, both are exploitative and oppressive in nature. The oppressive and exploitative structures of relations are mutually reinforced and maintained by the dominant and submissive groups manifest insecurity of the self who exercises it. They reflect on the low self-esteem of the person, hence lack of awareness, acceptance, respect and love of self.

The women and men of spirit who are free from the acquired consciousness do not need institutionalised religions with a set of rules because they live the religion in spirit and concretise it in their flesh and blood. When one is free from the acquired consciousness one feels ashamed of the illusion of having power to control the 'other'.

THE SPIRIT KNOWS WHAT IS IT TO BE HUMAN
IT KNOWS THE TRUTH
IT KNOWS TO LOVE
TO LIVE IN SPIRIT ONE SHOULD BE FREE
FROM ACQUIRED CONSCIOUSNESS.

IDENTIFICATION WITH THE OPPRESSOR

In fact, both the oppressed and the oppressor patterns are within the submissive and dominant individuals or groups. Both the attitudes and behaviour are internalised during the process of growth. Both the behaviour are learnt in order to take care of the being. there is not a human being on earth who likes to be submissive and be silent when she or he is oppressed and exploited by another human being or unjustly discriminated against. The behaviour is only used as a survival technique or to ward off greater danger or unpleasantness, which the ego is not yet ready to face. Fear, insecurity and at times prudence are the basic determining factors.

The following figure explains how oppressive behaviour is imbibed and made part of ones ego.

> Experience of resentment within while silently accepting the impostition of ideology or action by the dominant individual, group or the oppressor.

↓

> A wish to have the power of self-determination. Appreciation of the oppressor because the oppressor seems to be powerful.

↓

> A desire to possess what the oppressor has. A wish to control the oppressor and others, in other words to be like oppressor. i.e. identification with the oppressor.

↓

> Incorporation of the behaviour by which the other (the oppressor) seems to have dealt effectively and take care of herself/himself.

Thus the individuals and groups who seem to be submissive and silent or are oppressed have the oppressor within them. And when there is a suitable opportunity, oppressive behaviour is expressed by the oppressed. Similarly, the oppressor also has the internalised behaviours of dominance and submissiveness. That is why we find that an individual or a group may be submissive or dominant with different persons at the same time or with the same person at different times.

Some examples are listed below :

Example 1. A man from the oppressed group may be submissive with his landlord or master; however when he goes home, he can be cruel and oppressive towards his wife and children.

Example 2. A woman who is submissive to her husband may be aggressive with her subordinates.

Example 3. woman who has accepted a 'stereotyped role based on gender'and who carries on the functions of being a very submissive wife, may not even be aware that internally she is resenting it. She may passively or, at times, even explicitly, become oppressive and exploitative to her husband.

Mostly the key aspect to remember is that being dominant or submissive is a power game. They are also two sides of the same coin. If a person becomes submissive at some point of time then that person is also capable of being oppressive and dominant in another situation and vice versa, like the vacillations of a pendulum. The players may play them either consciously or unconsciously. They are either survival techniques or strategies to achieve some other goal. It is a game of how and who wields more power in order to control the other. They are stereotyped behaviours and those who engage in them are highly conditioned to play them and they are like prisoners. When one becomes self- aware then one can be free from them. Then one learns to experience power within, without being either dominant or subissive, then one moves towards internal freedom and growth.

There is a shared relationship between the oppressor and the oppressed. Often both are responsible for mutually reinforcing the patterns of behaviour in each other, because both have self interest.

For example, by being oppressive and exploitative the oppressor may have economic or material gain, may want the power of controlling others, may not be aware that she/he is pampering an inner insecurity. Similarly, there may be various reasons to be submissive, like survival, security, avoidance of responsibility, wanting appreciation, wanting sympathy or emotional dependency, material gain, avoiding pain of growth; being submissive also may be simply another strategy for controlling.

Change cannot be brought about unless there is change in thinking and attitudes, in at least one of the two, oppressor or oppressed. This ultimately means more self-awareness and a change in self-esteem, a refusal to be a partner in a relationship which blocks growth. The counter-culture being created through certain grass root actions and movements by the Dalits is an example of their growing self-awareness, leading to demand for change in defferent aspects of relationship with the dominant froups. This though painful at times, initiates a new dialogue with the established patterns.

THE DEVELOPMENT OF EGO BOUNDARY

A boundary defines a thing or a system. It delineates the elements belonging to the system and its environment. A system can be considered as a set of units or objects together with the relationships between the units and between their attributes. The boundary becomes visible due to a higher level of interaction between the units compared to the units outside the system. For example, a family is a system having its own boundary. The members of the family are the units with their own characteristics and uniqueness. The relationships between the members of the family and between the characteristics of each member makes every family a unique living system.

An individual, though a unit with relation to the family system, when considered separately, is also a system. The boundary between the individual (or organism) and the environment is more or less experienced by as what is inside and outside the skin. However, our skin in not a fixed armour. It breathes and touches.

The ego boundary is basically the differentiation of self and otherness and this differentiation is important. In this chapter we are going to explore:

(1) the process by which ego boundary develops; and

(2) experience of ego boundary: indetification and alienation.

The Process of Development of Ego-boundary :

From dependence to Independence: Human beings are born helpless, entirely dependent on the 'other.' By the 'other' is meant people who take care of the new born shild, until the child learns to look after herself. These significant people in an individual's life may be blood related or not relatd, though usually they are parents and siblings.

The development of ego boundaries is a process that continues through childhood into adulthood. During the early years the boundaries are more physical, but those established in later years are psychic in nature. During the early stages of growth the child does not differentiate between self and her/his envirnoment. Gradually, the child learns to differentiate herself/himself from others.

The ego begins with the child's ability to perceive her/his body as distinct from the external world. From this point, the person is able to see reality as subjective and objective. However, the person may not be still able to distinguish her/his own internal experiences from those of her/his dear ones. She/He will have to go through a great deal of struggle before distinguishing that her/his wish may be differet from the command of her/his parents. When chlidren are encouraged to express freely their thoughts, feelings, desires and wishes (whether those wishes are met or not) may find it easier to differentiate their inner experiences from outer. When children are expected to be obedient and submissive, not allowed to express themelves and not allowed to think for themselves may find themselves in confusion and painful struggles while differentiating themdelves from the environment, specially from the parents or older siblings.

In a culture where women's wishes are suppressed right from childhood and they are expected to fit into a particular stereotype model the girl children may find it more complex to know themselves as a separate identity. This is because of her environmental conditions where the girl is prevented from organising her own internal energies and development of a strong ego. The development of a strong ego would mean achieving the capacity of self-determination.

During seminars I am often reminded by people that it is the mother who teaches the daughter to conform to the stereotype roles. It does not really matter who does it, since we are not trying to blame anybody. We are only trying to understand the phenomenon. Mostly it is the prevalent thought with regard to gender roles determines the formation of young girls. Mother, father, brothers, or sisters are instruments to deliver it. Mostly mothers are also under pressure from significant others to shape their daughters in a particular way otherwise have to undergo a lot of criticism. However there are conscientious mothers/fathers who inspite of the criticism and pressure from significant others raise their daughters according to their own convictions.

Hence by developing one's own boundaries, there is another dimension added to the person, and that is the need for self- determination. The need for self-determination is first of all expressed when the person begins to differentiate from the dear ones. She or he perceives that one's needs, desires and experiences are unique and different even from one's dear ones and close friends. It is gradually manifested as the desire for superiority, for acquisition, for exploration, and for achievement, self-expression and lovingness.

It is important that every human being has the opportunity to differentiate oneself from the other and to develop a strong ego learns to deal with the environment and executes functions on behalf of the individual. When this opportunity is not there the person feels suffocated, suppressed and the persons energy then gets blocked and does not flow freely. This in turn blocks the person's capacities to express herself freely, to create, to enjoy life and to achieve the goals which actually one is capable of achieving.

The ego is, above all, a process and not a thing. It is best defined as a group of functions with a history in terms of early beginnings and subsequent growth. The essence of the ego is striving to master, to integrate and to make sense of experience. The growth of ego boundary is a process; it is not formed once for all. Hence, the ego boundary is, at first, very diffused. It grows in clarity as the person attains independence, individuality and uniqueness. In other words, the person tries to reach autonomy.

The trend toward autonomy consists of the expansion of the organism by assimilating and mastering the envirnoment. It is analogous to an egoistic drive in which the person attempts to satisfy craving and advance interest by modifying the environment to her needs.

The processes by which the internal world is built up and by which structure within the ego is consolidated are called internalisation. The intrapsychic preservation of the external objects takes place through internalisation. It is a process by which the person organises a part of ones energy and develops new patterns of expression of the ego in order to be more efficient and effective to take care of the being. Though this process is generally unconscious it may be conscious in highly developed human beings who are self aware. There are three different processes by which internalisation may take place: (a) incorporation (b) introjection and (c) identification.

(a) Incorporation: The object loses its distinct status as object and is assumed into the person's inner world. For example, let us consider a man who loves gardening. His garden means a lot to him. He has invested his energy and time in it and committed himself to it. This is a process of cathexis. He has invested energy in an object outside of himself. He becomes attached to it, and in order to nurture the plants, he learns a great deal about gardening, soil, fertilisers and pruning. when we cathect an object outside of ourselves we also incorporate a representation of that object into ourselves. So this process involves extension of one's limits or ego boundaries. The object becomes a part of the extended ego of the person.

(b) Introjection: By this mechanism the qualities of the person who was the center of the gratifying relationship are internalised and re-established as part of the organisation of the self. For example, children internalize those aspects of the parents which they think would help them in dealing successfully with the environment. The values as well as behaviour, both are internalised. In the beginning of an infant's life the people closest to her become her models.

(c) Indentification: This is a structuralising process that takes place within the ego, by which the ego constructs the inner constituents of regulatory control on the basis of selected elements derived from the model. It should not be mistaken for a simple imitation of the model. In this process, the person identifies with the model and internalises those aspects which are appreciated, which ultimately become part of the person.

The human organism is endowed with biological potentialities and capacities. Given the biological foundation, the ego arises out of the socio-cultural influences with which an individual has to interact constantly. The child internalises the norms and ideals of the group in which she or he grows and thereby becomes a functioning member of society. That is why family plays an important role in the growth and development of children.

The norms of society, largely patterns of dominance-submission, radicalism-conservatism and dependence-independence, have their genesis in the early parent-child relationship. However, they are not to be taken as permanent patterns in a person's life. When the person gains understanding of her own ego boundary and patterns of behaviours, then there is a possibility of choosing what she wants and letting go what one does not want. This means that life is a continuous journey of formation and transformation of self, offering and discovering new gifts for loving. The self keeps on flowing just as you cannot put your foot twice in the same flowing water you cannot meet the same person twice.

EVERY PERSON WHO IS ALIVE IS
PART OF A GREAT MOVEMENT OF LIFE
SO WE KEEP ON FLOWING.

The life force within a person keeps on flowing. For example, in almost every new born baby there is a tendency to be healthy, an impulse towards growth, or towards the actualisation of human potentialities; that is why we find children are best explorers.

Thus, leading to move from dependence to independence is a part of human growth. In this journey of life towards growth an individual constantly has to make decisions and choices. The process of making decision and choices requires a person to explore, to gain information and to develop skill. It means that the person needs to adapt constantly to changing situations. The developing ego is highly adaptive in nature and strives towards differentiation and integration. Through deiiferentiation the ego not only develops new adaptive skills but also specific ones. Through integration the ego achieves a kind of economy, combining various adaptive skills to make new ones. This involves a series of trials and errors through which an individual develops her own patterns of behaviours. These patterns give the person a sense of uniqueness and identity. Thus development of ego boundary is accompanined by the process of attaining a stable and enduring concept of self-identity. That is, the person develops a frame of reference.

COGNITIVE MAP

Human beings need to have a frame of reference, a stable and consitent way of perceiving and comprehending the world. This involes a set of assumtions a person makes about herself and her world concerning: (a) Reality as the person thinks it is. This is a view of things as the person thinks they really are, of the kind of person she is and of the nature of the world; (b) Possibility-the view of how things could be the possibilities of change; and (c) Value the view of how things should be. This set of assumptions provides the "inner cognitive map" or "model of reality" which determines how a person perceives reality and behaves.

Based on the perception of reality, human beings construct models of experience. The activity of building a model or inner cognitive map has a basis in the psycho-biological processes. In this process we cannot escape the limitations of our biological origins. We do not perceive reality as it is. Carl Jung observes that " Man ... never perceives anything fully or completely. He can see, hear, touch, taste, but how far he sees, how well he hears, what his touch tells him, and what he taste depends upon the number and quality of his senses .... No matter what instruments he uses, at some point he reaches the edge of certainty beyond which conscious knowledge cannot pass," Human beings are limited; hence the grasp pf reality is partial.

Our perceptions form the basis of our models of the world and there is a difference in the perception of each individual, which necessarily means that there are variations in the cognitive map of each person. There are also built in errors in our models which can limit our growth. It is just like the case of a person withan erroneous map who reaches a worng place and becomes miserable.

There are three mechanisms common to all model building activities: (a) generalisation, (b) deletion and (c) distortion. Bandler and Grinder call these three the 'universal human modelling processes'. They determine our abilities to: focus, plan, learn, act and dream.

(a) **Generalisation** : Many times we do not need to learn new concepts or behaviours from scratch. This is because at least some components of them have been experienced previously. For example, one who knows cycling can easily learn to ride a motor cycle. This ability to generalise helps us to economise energy and eliminate the need of relearning. It is important to realise that model-building processes have both advantages and disadvantages. For example, if a person bitten by a dog generalises that all the dogs are dangerous, then life becomes difficult. Or, if women generalise based on some incidents, that all men are either rapists or batterers of women, that is an unrealistic generalisation based on distorted perception.

(b) **Deletion** : Our central nervous system screens information, allowing us to function at peak efficiency. The nervous system is flooded with information through the senses every second; if no screening takes place, human beings would be a confused lot, without the energy for important work. Our ability to delete is very important for our survival. However, the same process can create serious limitations; we are tuned to pay attention only to what we want. For example, if I have a belief that certain person is manipulative, then I may be sensitive to the times when he is manipulative and may leave out other kinds of that person's behaviour which might be important in under-standing the whole person.

(c) **Distortion :** It is a process by which we alter perception. Using this process we can dream, fantasise and also interpret a piece of art and enjoy it. However, this process can also cause a lot of pain and suffering. For example, if a man sees his wife talking to another man and interprets that she does not love him any more; or, just because literacy is useful, if we perceive that illiterates are useless, then this is a distorted perception.

The development of this frame of reference depends to a large extent on the culture of a community. Culture may be defined as " that complex whole which includes knowledge belief, art, morals, laws, customs and any other capabilities and habits acquired by man as a member of society." (Tylor 1871) The definition of culture given by Goodenough (1963) includes "organisation of experience" shared by members of a community, including" their standards for perceiving, predicting, judging and acting." It means that culture includes all socially standardised ways of seeing and thinking about the world; of understanding relationships among people, things and events; of establishing preferences and purpose; of carrying our actions and pursuing goals. The structure of institutions and culture are dependent on each other.

The set of beliefs imparted through religion, the way of living of the group or community to which the individual belongs to, the culture of the other communities to which one is exposed, the values around which society is organised and the trends of development in a society influence the person. A person is exposed to the beliefs, values and norms first and foremost in the family, then through neighbours, school and friends. That does not mean that an individual receives ready made meaning through organised experience of the previous and contemporary generation. Each individual builds her own model of understanding, interpreting and giving meaning to the reality around, based on her own perceptions and experience, in a way that is meaningful to her existence.

The specific manifestations of needs and the actual ways in which a person realises inner potentialities are determined by the social arrangements under which the individual lives. A person also develops in accordance with the opportunities that a particular society offers to her. She develops a social character in keeping with the requirements of the society. An individual attempts to gain personal indentity, tries to develop rootedness in the circle by network of relationships like family, friends and wider circle by developing a life style which is not only acceptable but also favourably redgarded. This is a very decisive point; many people dedicate their lives to actualising a concept or an image of what they should be like, rather than actualising themselves. That is why few people have a self and most people have a void, because they are busy projecting themselves as this or that.

The less confident we are in ourselcves, the less we are in touch with ourselves and the world, the more we want to control others, and we become more intolerant towards uncertainty. If you let the situation guide your action, then you learn to cope, to develop inner resources. In other words, a person's adjustment to society usally represents a compromise between inner needs and outer demands. The process might frustrate the person.

EXPERIENCE OF EGO BOUNDARIES

The phenomena of ego boundary are identification and alienation,

Indentification :

I identify myself at a given moment through all that I am aware of and experience myself: my movements:

physical, emotional and thought processes; my needs: physical, psychological and spiritual; and in relation to otherness, Generally people also identify themselves with what they have: wealth, influence, position and even their profession. When these are taken away from them, they feel they don't exist any more; some may even commit suicide. We are easily identified with our families, friends, clan, in India, also with caste. They become our ego extensions. If anyone of them is hurt, then we too experience the same. Within the boundary we experience security and familiarity. People who perceive the world outside themselves as hostile, unnurturing and confusing like to remain inside the boundaries. And it can be lonely behind these boundaries. Such people find a kind of safety in their loneliness.

The boundary is not a closed fortress. The boundary between ME and YOU is an ever changing boundary where two people meet. The process of encounter changes people unless the person is already pigeon holed and has developed a social character. Then the boundary can be become rigid. When two people are in love the ego boundary expands and becomes an 'us' boundary. However the dimension of love is usually misunderstood. We donot usually love a person. That is very rare. We love a certain property in that person which is identical with our behaviour or supplements our behaviours. We think we are in love with the total person and when we encounter the aspect which we abhor we do not say" this aspect of yours is disgusting and the other part is lovable." We say, "You are disgusting; get out of my life."

The act of being in love can be a spontaneous process taking place through attraction, what is generally called as 'falling in love'. In this the ego boundaries collapse temporarily which is experienced as ecstasy. A bonding between two people takes place. The bond may be temporary or lasting one. The partners experience the temporary merging with the other and in those moments feel they can over come any obstacles. They experience the unlimitedness of their limits. When they confront reality then they get back to their limits, i.e. the ego boundaries snap back into their place and then they fall out of love. This is not really love. Love, in fact, can exists in a context where people may not fall in love but be in love by deciding to be so. It requires a decision, a commitment. It is commitment to extend oneself for the nurturing of the well being of self and others. By ' well being; I mean the 'spiritual growth' of the person.

As a person matures and experiences oneness with the whole of creation and with humanity, she finds that this experience is qualitatively different from the experience of falling in love. It is a mystical union, what Abraham Maslow refers to as the 'plateau experience.' In this process there is extension of one's boundaries. The extension of one's limits requires effort. Real love therefore is an experience of enlargement of self. When there is enlargement of self the boundary becomes thinner. This is the outcome of a process of many years of loving.

The person is then able to transcend the self. One of the dimensions of transcendence is being able to accept the difference of other people without expecting them to change, being able to identify with people when they are very different from us. In the process of self-transcendence one is simultaneously inside and outside the boundary. There are religions which belives that a child does not have an ego boundary and spontaneously identifies herself with the whole world, and that is the original unity we must achieve. I sense that the development of ego boundary, in other words, the developments of self, is important. In order to transcend oneself one must first of all have a self.

Alienation :

This is due to experiencing self as more precious than otherness. It means separating oneself from others and giving importance to self at the cost of others. It is also due to taking unlikeness very much for granted. When there is alienation, then we come to the problem of hostility, rejection-pushing away.

Hate is a function of kicking somebody out of the boundary for something, and is referred to as disowning or alienation. When a person's existence is a threat to us for some reason or other, then we want to exclude the person from our ego boundary, from ourselves, we want to annihilate the person. For example, when you buy a piece of land, the first thing that you do if you have resources is to put up a wall, a boundary. You do not want people to trespass and if you do not like someone, then you do not want that person to come home. Similarly, when some of our thoughts or/and feelings are unpleasant or unacceptable to us, family, community of society, then too we want to disown them. We repress them and try to remain intact superficially at the cost of disowning many valuable parts of ourselves. " Me angry with you ? never it is just a pattern " "Me attracted towards you ? never it is just my way of interacting with people" Hence a very small part of our energy becomes available to us an our ego boundary shrinks. This is because we are a co-ordination and different bits or parts add to the energy system. So when we disown any part of the self we become smaller and smaller, we become less in touch with ourselves. Our ability to live decreases, we become more rigid and allow ourselves only to cope as our character, as our preconceived pattern prescribes it. It does not help the person to unfold herself.

The ego boundary is a natural phenomenon and it applies to every situation of life. Now let's say you are feminist or you are for the equality of dalits then you tend to consider the others, who are not in the camp, outside the boundary as bad people. And closer the boundary defences, greater the chance of clashes, hostility or wars.

There can be ideological boundaries, people professing to be communists or free enterprisers. The development of a person's ideology depends to a large extent on the socio-cultural, politico-economic and spiritual dimensions of the existing reality. Ideolgies provide a set of assumptions or belifes based on which one interprets reality. It is expressed through social institutions, hence it is not only ideational but also has the component of action. Ideologies are articulated by human beings and ideologies form individuals and groups. For example, the ideological aspect that 'only Aryans have divinity' made Hitler a tyrant. Similarly, the Greeks perceived themselves as aristocrats and despised the rest of the world. Ideologies influence the consciousness of individuals and the collective consciosness of the member of a society. people outside my ideology are bad people, so I can hate, kill and vent my aggression. I can remain intact by rationalising or justifying my action with the help of my ideology. If you have a perspective, and can see large outlook, you seem to be more fair, objective and balanced.

Human consciousness is formed through ideological means. The social structures that we create reflect on human consciouseness.

There is a corelation between the mechanisms that foster alienation and supersession in society. Groups of people are marginalised and their world views are not taken in to account when social structures are created. These groups of people are pused to the periphery. Those whose views are taken into account are the main stream. The different structures of alienation, economic, political and ideological, are interrelated. What we also see these days is the economic structures of alienation are gradually becoming stronger and playing a basic role in the alienation of groups of people. Hence economic alienation is original and primordial, while the others are only derivative.

However in India, the untouchable groups are also economically pushed to the periphery. Women are generally a group that is pushed to the periphery. They are also economically alienated.

Marx seems to ground his claim on the dialectic of consciousness and being. In contrast to Hegel who affirmed the primacy of consciousness over being, Marx held that it is being that determines conciousness. In the famous preface of 1859 Marx reaffirmed the following: "The mode of production of material life determines the general character of the social, political and spiritual processes of life. It is not consciousness of men determines their being, on the contrary, their social being determines their consciousness ..... With the change of the economic foundation the entire immense superstructure is more or less transformed." Probably, in the context in which Marx existed, he could make sence of his reality based on the visible, social productive forces and exploitation of the proletariat in the name of God and religion, by giving supremacy to economic forces over anything else, since people do have the tendency to use religion as an opium. However, it gives a partial view of life.

In India, researchers as well as acting groups with a Marxist bent, have also applied the socio-economic categories to caste and gender, the problematics of which have wider roots. I am not proposing that the ideologies which have recognised the existence of transcendental, or, for that matter, even the immanent presence of God have been fair to untouchables and women. They have not considered the views of untouchables and women. The peripheral groups including women for a certain period of time in history, have accepted throgh silence the dominant ideology as absolute and organised their life based on the same. Now they are in the process of articulating that dominant ideology is oppressive for them and they are presenting their own ideologies in order to be free form oppression. However, ideologies are made by us and when they are taken as absolute, they become closed boundaries and liimt our perception and growth.

EXERCISES

Exercise : 1 Body Awareness

Lie down flat on your back on the ground.

Close your eyes.

Take three deep breaths.

As you breathe, be aware of the air going through your nostrils to your chest, stomach and abdomen.

Exhale slowly.

Now be aware of the toes of your right foot. Be aware of each one of them. Be aware of various sensations in the toes.

Be aware of your right foot.

Be aware of sensations in the right foot.

Be aware of your right leg.

Be aware of sensations in the right leg.

Be aware of your right buttock.

Be aware of sensations in the right buttock.

Now be aware of your left toes, be aware of sensations in the left toes. Be aware of your left foot, be aware of sensations in the left foot. Be aware of your left leg, be aware of sensations in the left leg.

Be aware of left buttock, be aware of sensations in the left buttock.

Keep breathing deeply and slowly.

Now be aware of sensations in your lower back.

Be aware of the sensations in your upper back.

Be aware of the sensations in your abdomen.

Be aware of the sensations in your stomach.

Be aware of the sensations in your chest.

Keep breathing deelply and slowly.

Now be aware of the palm of your right hand.

Be aware of the right hand.

Be aware of the palm of your left hand.

Be aware of the left hand.

Be aware of the right shoulder.

Be aware of the left shoulder.

Keep breathing deeply and slowly.

Be aware of the sensations in your neck.

Now be aware of your chin, jaws, lips, nose, eyes, ears, all the facial muscles and head.

Keep breathing deeply and slowly.

Now be aware of your entire body.

Exerices : 2 Awareness of Different Aspects of Self.

Remember many different contrasting situations in which your thoughts, feeling and behaviour differ sharply.

List the situations in which such contrasting feelings, thoughts and behaviour occurs.

Be as specific and concrete as you can in describing feelings, thoughts and behaviour in each situation.

See connection between thoughts, feeling and behaviour.

Be aware that this is part of your own energy being organised into a particular package of thoughts, feelings and behaviour.

Be aware of the conditioning to think, feel and behave in a certain manner in a particular situation.

AWARENESS OF YOUR THOUGHTS, FEELINGS
AND BEHAVIOUR IS ONE OF THE
FIRST STEPS TOWARDS TRANSFORMATION.
BE AWARE OF YOURSELF.
BE A WITNESS TO WHO YOU ARE.

Exercise : 3 Discovering Patterns

Make a list of similar situations which you have lived.

Be aware of thoughts, feelings and behaviour in these similar situations.

Be as specific as you can.

In these situations what similarities do you see in your thoughts, feelings and behaviour ?

Try to see the pattern in your behaviour.

Be aware of the personal gain through this behaviour.

Be aware how it blocks you.

Exercise : 4 Inner view

With an uncompromising honesty with yourself reflect on : your real self, social self and ideal self.

Real self :

How I think and behave in real self ?

How I feel about myself ?

How I enhance and defend myself ?

How I meet my needs ?

Social self :

Self as experienced by others

How do I make contact with others ?

How do I reach out to others ?

How much do I reveal myself to others ?

How open am I to the responses of others to me ?

How I evaluate and respond to the reactions of others ?

Am I reserved or outgoing ?

What kind of life style I have adapted or feel attracted towards ? Why ?

Ideal self :

What I would like to be as a person

What I want to feel and do

What goals I want to achieve ? Why ?

Exercise : 5 Awareness on the Need to Control Others

Lie down on your back or take a comfortable position and sit down.

Relax your body and keep breathing deeply and slowly.

Now be aware of relationships with other people in your life.

Be aware of specific situations in which you dominate others.

Be aware of specific situations in which you are submissive to others.

What do you understand about yourself through these patterns of interaction ?

Exercies : 6 Relationship with Self

Relax your body and mind by being aware of each part of your body. While doing this exercise keep breathing deeply and slowly.

With an uncompromising honesty with self reflect on:

Do I trust myself ?

Do I nurture myself ?

Do I share my feelings and thoughts with myself ?

Do I have fun with myself ?

Do I judge myself ?

Do I accept myself ?

Do I truly listen to my own thoughts ?

Do I spend quality time with myself ?

Do I give priority to be with myself ?

Am I committed to myself ?

Do I treat myself with respect ?

Do I accept ny feelings, whatever they might be ?

Do I love myself ?

Exercise : 7 Awareness on Core Beliefs

Relax your body and mind by being aware of each part of your body. While doing this exercise keep breathing deeply and slowly.

With an uncompromising honesty with yourself identify :

the core beliefs which you have about yourself that motivate your behaviour,

the core beliefs that you have about other people, that motivate your behaviour and guides your relationship with them. They may be dear ones, people of other culture, language, gender, caste, race and country.

the core beliefs about God or Power higher than human beings or Universe, that motivate your behaviour,

the core beliefs about earth and cosmos that motivate your behaviour toward them.

3

Transformation of Self

Human beings in this world learn to think, feel and behave in a certain way. In other words people get conditioned to live in particular way. This would mean we automatically tend to get into a rut. Though most of this process takes place unconsciously, part of it may also be conscious. When you are conditioned then you only have a partial view of life. It limits you from achieving what you want to achieve during this life time and blocks the way for joy, happiness, love and creativity. It gives an illusion that, that is the only way to be.

The transformation of a person takes place with the development of critical consciousness. The development of critical consciousness would mean that the person is on a journey of knowing about himself or herself more than before. This means you start becoming aware how you are conditioned to live life in a certain way. This awareness opens the door to the limitless possibilities of existence and allows you to bloom as a spiritual being, which is your real nature.

UNCOMPROMISING HONESTY WITH SELF IS THE DOOR TO THE PATH OF DISCOVERING LIMITLESSNESS OF SELF

DEVELOPMENT OF CRITICAL CONSCIOUSNESS

Development of critical consciousness makes a person critically aware of oneself and the structures in which one lives. Usually the development of critrical consciouseness is accompanied by increased self-awareness. The process of self-awareness makes the person aware of her conditioning.

In other words the person becomes aware of what consciously or unconsciously she or he internalised in order to survive, cope with the world or get what one wants in this life. In one way the conditoning helps the person, for example if you have learnt cycling ones then every time you want to cycle you do not have to learnt it newly. On the other hand it limits you because if we generalise and behave similarly in similar human encounters or similar problems then we loose opportunities for bringing out the best from us as well as others or loose opportunities for bringing about change and newness in life. Infact the conditioning can make a person repeat the past, instead of living life creatively and enjoying it. When a person is aware of the conditioning then one can make use of ones skills in human encounter discreetly and also become creative.

When there is increased self-awareness the person who previously accepted the belief, values and norms of society and organised oneself around it now tries to look at it more objectively. The goal of this examination is no more self-acceptance or rootedness in the family or society, but opening oneself for deeper meaning and truth. This is another phase of growth. During this phase it is possible for a person to feel that the ground on which one is standing is opening or disappearing and as if under the feet there is no ground at all. It may be an experience of falling in an abyss or being engulfed by a dark cloud of unknowing. The situation creates a sense of not knowing anything and not even knowing how to exist in this world. The person temporarily goes through a sense of great uncertainty and insecurity. Trust in oneself and Faith in God provide support and play a great role at this juncture.

FAITH IS FLYING THROUGH THE DARK CLOUDS WHERE NOTHING IS VISIBLE

This period of change may be painful since previously attained homoeostasis in relationships can be disturbed through new discoveries. Gradually the person may make a choice to have new beliefs based in the sense of direction of his or her life and may develop a new perspective of life. The new beliefs and values may be different from the beliefs and values of dear ones or friends. Generally during this period the dear ones and friends may get disturbed since they cannot make sense of this new situation. The person seems to have become unpredictable to them. They wish that the person should become like before and attempt to advise the person. There is a possibility for the newness in the person to create insecurity in them. This is because they also have to develop new ways to deal with and accommodate the person who has become new. There are possibilities of separation, isolation or breaking of relationships.

Critical consciousness does not develop uniformly among all people; it develops more in those peolpe who seek truth in all matters and struggle for it. While searching for truth it is not possible to take things, people and oneself for granted. As mentioned by Erich Fromm in "Escape from Freedom", people run away from it. Because he says growth can be painful and freedom is an inseparable aspect of growth. Goldstein tells us that a normal, healthy individual is one in whom the tendency towards self-actualisation acts from within, and overcomes the disturbance arising from the clash with the world. In this context the clash is due to the persons adherence to truth. When a person looks for truth, then his or her interactions are not guided by insecurity ,in the sense that the person does not say or do things to please the other. Usually, people try to please others when they are insecure and want to get "self acceptance" and gain 'self importance.'

Maslow also feels that many people are afraid of and draw back from becoming fully human or self-actualised. It means that in order to dream dreams and to take the consequences of actualising them, one must develop the capacity for bearing a high level of frustration. The frustration and unhappiness are not necessary conditions to actualise the dreams. One can work toward actualising the dreams and bear the consequences and also simultaneously choose to be happy. Being critically conscious about oneself helps a person to have the courage to be fully human, to be happy with the unfolding of her/his nature.

Attainment of this growth leads a person to make conscious decisions with regard to oneself or ones life hence the person also willingly accepts the reponsibility for his or her own life. Thus taking responsibility for one's action is an important growth aspect of the self in this phase no matter what the consequences are. Carl Rogers mentions the emergence of a new person "highly aware, space, scornful of the conformity of institutions and the dogma of authority."

Attaining critical consciousness is a continuous process of action and reflection. This process gradually increases the internal freedom of the person. It creates a sense of detachment in the person, helping the person 'let go' of pet ideas, beliefs and perceptions about people, and enabling the person to have new ones.

Human consciousness, though formed by ideological means, is capable of critique and transformation, because self also has the dimension of creativity. The concept of the creative self was first given by Alfred Adler. Sullivan also mentioned that ' human beings are not only unique and creative but also self-conscious.' According to Maslow, "as personality unfolds through maturation in a benign environment and by active efforts on the part of the person to realise their nature, the creative power of humans manifest themselves, ever more clearly. The increase of creativity is due to a person's expression of the 'experience of reality', which is accompanied by the person's growth into maturity. Both these aspects: self-consciousness and creativity are important for facilitating transformation.

Dominant groups in any society impose their own conception of reality on subordinate groups. As self-awareness grows and critical consciousness is formed, the oppressed become capable to create alternative cultural and political institutions, to establish their own understanding of oppression in order to oppose and change it. Articulation of experienced oppression and resistance to oppression are important aspects of the process of bringing about change. This process helps people to raise their level of consciousness. when people with a raised level of consciousness interact with other people, institutions and society at large there will be a snowball effect.

There is a dialectic relationship between individual consciousness and structural determinants. Resistance is an important part of the process of growth. It is not only the oppressed group that resists the imposition of the dominant group ideology; but the dominant persons or/and groups also resist the counter. Culture expressed by the oppressed groups. This struggle is an important aspect of the growth of the dominant and the submissive. The critical consciousness of human beings grows in the process of self-evaluation, interaction with social structures, and by reflecting on the physical environment with an uncompromising honesty with self.

The oppressive and exploitative dimensions which are embedded in our socio-economic structures are also present within every individual as part of the self. That is why the processes of 'self transformation' and 'social transformation' feed and support each other. That is why a person who wants to work for 'justice' and 'social transformation' needs to be critically aware of herself and must also be prepared for transformation within.

Movement and change are possible due to the critical consciousness of human beings which gets involved in a process of dialectics with the world. In this process human consciousness constructs and reconstructs meaning and searches for truth. The human critical consciousness is instrumental in discovering the force of hegemony in one's own consciousness. It also becomes the voice within oneself.

The unknown author of the Cloud of Unknowing advises the follower of Christ to " strain every nerve in every possible way to know and experience yourself, as you really are. It will not be long, I suspect, before you have a real knowledge and experience of God as he is." The more a person's critical consciousness is developed, the more that person is enabled to identify the unjust structures within and outside, to initiate a process to deal with them and hence increase internal freedom. This would, in turn, facilitate a process of having more fulffilling relationships with people; more energy would then be available; for creativity. Every human being has a need to move in that direction; Maslow called it the need for 'self-actualisation'. A critically conscious person is aware of the inner and outer. In the words of Carl Rogers we can say that," The whole person is one who is completely open to the data from internal world."

There is an aspect of self which is present throughout as an observer within us, the reality which observes everything that we do. This is the aspect which facilitates the development of critical consciousness. When there is a realisation that observer and the observed are the same, the integration of different aspects 'the observer' and 'the observed', takes place. As also pointed out by J. Krishnamurthi, the conditioning, that is, one's mind being disposed in a certain way, dissolves with the realisation and the person with this realisation is different from the energy and activity of conditioning. It makes the person experience emptiness, void, nothingness or stillness. The mind is usually not used to keeping still, subordinate to the 'being'. Being is the organism. Experiencing stillness is being in touch with existence. It is also knowing the 'organism' as one experiences it.

INDEPENDENCE TO INTERDEPENDENCE

An important growth aspect of this phase is moving from 'independence to interdependence'. Growth consists in moving from the dependency of infancy towards the independence of adulthood. Growing into an independent adult is necessary for the development of self.

However, there is another dimension of growth, going out of oneself from independence to interdepndence. Growing from independence to interdepence requires an inner journey and stripping of oneself in order to freely give onself to others and accept interdependence without the interference of one's pride and arrogance. It means acceptance of one's strengths and limitations, familiarity with one's insecuritiues and fears. It also means acceptance of the other, and becoming more and more 'other conscious'. In fact growth is only accepting reality by gaining deeper awareness of it. It is a beginning of the recognition of the oneness of all creation.

The average person in today's society gets stuck with the struggle of wanting to be independent and moving out from the state of dependency. This is due to the set of values received from the existing organisation of society and the ideology of our institutions. Attaining 'indpendence' is an important stage in the development of humankind; however, we need to move forward into realising interdependence as a concrete reality for human beings.

When Erikson emphasises the growth of a healthy and integrate person, it has many implications for spitual development; it is a focus on human possibilities. There is also a focus on possible psycho-social develpoment of people; in fact the psycho-social development of people and spiritual growth are integrated. For example, one cannot be not seeking truth and/or be very selfish and at the same time be very spiritual. Being spiritual necessarily means 'being a lover'. Love includes the 'faith dimension' because love is the capacity to discern. Loving is discerning to have more life. Love and life come from God.

The faith dimension emphasises the interdependence of human beings on one another. When a person becomes fragmented, the role of friends, family and community are important in the healing process. When people begin to see the deeper reality and strength, the virtues of the different stages of psychosocial development given by Erikson one begins to see the spiritual unfoldment beneath the surface. For example, accepting interdependence of all would also mean deepening of the 'basic trust' in oneself and others.

One must neither dominate nor be submissive in order to be free or to accept interdependence. A child, for example, is free not because it accepts interdependence but because it can smile at anyone without malice. However, the child is self-centered, in the sense that the other does not exist for the child; it thinks of everyone in terms of self. Hence growing into self-consciousness and other- centeredness and unfolding into a self are necessary, but in this process certain beliefs, values and norms, which are internalised from the dominating exploitative and oppresssive trends of the society, become a block for accepting interdependence and for the growth of self. For example:

1. The trend of over-consumption can make a person insensitive to others' and the environment.

2. The caste structure can make people insensitive to their own and others humanity.

3. The gender bias can dehumanise both men and women.

It is important to recognise these in oneself and shed them from onself, and be childlike again without any pretensions about oneself. Generally, people like to cling to them, however crippling it is for growth since it gives them a sense of security, however false. Human beings posses the potential for attaining internal freedom, yet in order to actualise this potential one must have uncompromising honesty with oneself, a desire to grow, which means a desire for the spirit of truth; in reality this is possible only when a person truly loves oneself. It reminds me of the following poem by M. C. Richards, from Poetry and the Person:

'From the seed grows a root, then a sprout; from the sprout, the seedling leaves; from the leaves, the stem; around the stem, the branches; at the top the flower ..... We cannot say that the seed causes the growth, nor that the soil does. We can say that the potentialities for growth lie within the seed, mysterious life forces, which, when properly fostered, take on certain forms."

SPIRITUAL DIMENSION

Human beings by nature are spiritual beings. The spiritual dimension of our nature is present at the very beginning of life. Christian spirituality includes every dimension of human life. Christian spirituality involves the human capacity of self- transcending knowledge, love and commitment as it is actualised through the experience of God, by the gift of the spirit. That is why spiritual development involves every dimension of human life and total development.

The spiritual dimension of the self facilitates the creation of wholeness in a person. It integrates different aspects of the self. Carl Rogers writes, "The basic tendency of growth to actualise and expand oneself-is seen to best advantage when an individual is observed over a long period of time. There is a forward movement in the life of every person." Rogers further writes," The forward moving tendency can only operate when choices are clearly perceived and adequately symbolised. A person cannot actualise him or herself unless one is able to discriminate between progressive and regressive ways of behaving."

This dimension is part of the ability to discern to have more life.

Rogers was also of the opinion that the actualising tendency of an individual is selective, paying attention only to those aspects of the envionment that promise to move the person constructively in the direction of fulfilment and wholeness. Roger seems to have stumbled upon an important aspect of the life of human beings, that is, that the unfolding of human potentialities seem to occur in a certain direction of growth and the decision making capacity of an individual moves in the direction which gives more life and wholeness.

According to Jung, development is an unfolding of the original undifferentiated wholeness with which humans are born. In order to develop into an integrated person every system must be permitted to reach the fullest degree of differentiation. Jung refers to this process of disclosure of self as individuation.

When diversity has been achieved by the operation of the individuation process, the differentiated systems are then integrated by the transcendent function. It is endowed with the capacity to unite all of the opposing trends of the several systems and to work towards the ideal goal of perfect wholeness. The unconscious expression of a desire for wholeness is found in dreams, myths and other symbolic representations. Eric Fromm also felt that human beings have an urge for relatedness and transcendence. The urge is manifested from within when the potentiality exists. Solitude, relatedness, wholeness and transcendence are important aspects of human life.

Human development from childhood to adulthood is a journey of continuous unfolding of the potentialities, becoming more and more differentiated and complex. This process of growth also involves deepening of consciousness of self, society, physical environment and ultimately reaching higher levels of consciousness. Our present conscious mind is very limited. After the person reaches a certain level of critical consciousness, the further growth of the person consists of integration within and moving from highly differentiated state towards wholeness. Even in this state the growth is not complete. There are many more potentialities endowed on human nature, which is created in the image and likeness of God. For example, Ken Wilber has gone much beyond Jung while speaking about the spectrum of human consciousness. We can see them as the possibilities of the self in the process of becoming. It is a process of action and reflection.

It is that spiritual dimension manifests itself as a first stage of human development; rather it is present throughout the life of an individual, expressed concretely in relationship with oneself, other people and nature. Love is the transcending principle which facilitates the strengthening and growth of this dimension. At the being level it is experienced as joyous lovingness.

The whole journey of human life can be explained as a journey of learning to love and experience love, and at each stage, moving towards a greater depth of love. The journey reveals a lot of human nature and the purpose of human life and creation. It is also a painful journey, where one has to learn not to run away from pain and commitment to love.

Every stage of loving takes a person deeper within oneself and the reality around. However, a careful reflection of the process as experienced by a person introduces the person to the true nature of humanity and oneness of humanity, nature and God.

INTERDEPENDENCE TO INTERCONNECTEDNESS

When the person gains insights into the real nature of human beings he or she learns that the whole creation is connected. Our perception of separation is only an illusion.

There is only one ground reality and we are part of that ground reality. We are 'one body'.

Hence we are part as well as whole. Just like a drop ot water in the Ocean is Ocean itself, when it is aware of the Ocean, otherwise it is merely a drop of water. Of course the drop of water has all the qualities of water but it does not have the qualities of the Ocean. Hence it will exist merely as water and not as Ocean.

Exercise : 8 Contemplation on Who Am I ?

Be seated in a comfortable position

Be aware of your breathing

Feel the air as it enters your nostrils

Feel the expansion and contractions in your body when you inhale and exhale air.

Be aware of the rhythm in your breathing, do not try to change or control, only be aware.

Now be aware of your feelings. Do not strugle with them in any way. Do not try to change them or control them. Only be aware of them. do not try to hold them or cling to them.

Now be aware of your thoughts.

Do not judge, edit, control the sensations. Only be aware of them.

Let them come and go.

Now be aware of sensations in your body.

Do not judge, edit, control the sensations. Only be aware of them.

The feeling, thoughts, and sensations keep on changing. They come and go like the passing clouds.

Are you the feelings, thoughts or sensations ?
Who are you ?

Exercise : 9 Meditation on Body of Light

Lie down flat on the ground on your back.

Be aware of your breathing.

Take three deep breaths.

When you exhale, let go all the air from the abdomen.

Now visualise a bright white light at the center of your body, that is near your heart.

Now let this light move into your entire left leg.

Visualise the entire left leg as made up of white light.

Now visualise this light move into your entire right leg.

Visualise the entire right leg as made up of White light.

Now visualise this light moving into your entire back, abdomen stomach and chest.

Now let the light extend into your left arm and then right arm.

Let the light extend into your neck, face and entire head,

Now feel and visualise your entire body as made up of light.

Now feel the light extending beyond your body.

Feel your light extending and joining the light outside your boundary.

Where does your light end and outside light begin ?

4
Healing Journey

'Now' is the time for the whole creation to be healed. The planet earth is crying with a longing to be healed. Human beings have the power to heal when they allow themselves to be healed. They must utter the 'mantra', that is 'the thought' to be healed. 'Now' is the precious time. 'Now' is eternity.

The prayer for healing is indeed a cry for new birth, a new order. The whole creation i. e., the macrocosm and every individual soul, i. e., the microcosm are longing for a new birth. There is suffering and pain around and we want to be healed. We want to become instruments of healing.

Violence breeds violence. Disease creates more illness. Unhappiness breeds unhappiness. If you want to be healed then be a healer yourself. In this situation I sense it is fitting to quote Hildegarde Bingen:

Now in the People

that were meant to be green,

there is no more life of any kind,

There is only shrivelled barren

The winds are burdened by the utterly awful stink of evil,

Selfish goings-on.

Thunderstorms menace. The air belches out the filthy uncleanliness of the peoples.

The earth should not be injured

The earth must not be destroyed

Humanity is meant to be a blessing for the whole creation but the same humanity also has the power to destroy the earth. People who are meant to be green are not because they have 'chosen' to be barren. Hence there is simultaneous existence of rich natural resources and extremes of misery and poverty. We have to bless the earth and 'let it be.' But we have chosen a life style of hoarding and clinging. How would it be if each drop of Ocean felt that it exists separately from rest of the Ocean. And if each drop of Ocean feels that it must destroy the other drops so that it can exist.

Presently there is disorientation and violence of all kinds. The statistics tell us that there is criminal offence against women every seven minutes, a molestation every 26 minutes, and act of cruelty every 33 minutes, a kidnap or abduction every 43 minutes, an act of sexual harassment every 51 minutes, a rape every 54 minutes, a dowry death every one hour and 42 minutes. We know that the life style of the present generation has been consuming all the natural resources, destroying life and polluting the atmosphere, leading towards the suicide of the whole creation.We have not been working towards giving an alternative life giving perspective to our younger generation. Yet all of us agree that the earth must not be destroyed because there is still hope. We can be healed and be instruments of healing.

ABOUT HEALING

The earth itself is ruptured and torn apart when there is injustice and imbalance in relationships. This is expressed in the dualism of subject/object fashion of relationships with others and earth. It leads to manipulation and control. Exercise of control in relationships indicates lack of growth. Oppressive relationships dehumanise the oppressor and acceptance of control dehumanises the oppressed. Then we hear the voice of Yahweh speaking, " I have heard the cries of my people."

The return of justice and balance in relationships is healing for humankind. Today, a number of relationships need healing. The relationships between women and men, between people of different religions, cultures, languages, races and castes, between rich and poor, also between the mainstream and people with certain illnesses like AIDS and the mentally ill, those who are able- bodied and physically and mentally handicapped, literates and illiterates.

We must allow relationships to heal because personal salvation is not salvific. When we are in deep communion with others the relationships facilitate healing. Relationships constitute part of healing of every person.

The enlightened pepole of our society like Jesus, Buddha and Basavanna to state a few, broke the barriers in relationships among different groups of people. They interacted freely and openly with prostitutes, those who were considered sinners and other excommunicates of society. They showed compassion to both the mainstream and those who were pushed to the periphery of society. By doing this they healed division and brought integration to humanity and to the rest of the creation.

One of the greatest sins of omission is not falling in love with life. It is greatest because it is at the root of all evil. The awakening of love, i.e. being in love with life, is healing for humankind. Being in love with life also means responding to God's dreams for us. This means experiencing the beauty and to be beautiful again. As Meister Ekhart puts it, "This then is salvation: to marvel at the beauty of created things and praise the beautiful providence of their Creator."

When religions ask people to withdraw from life and when it shapes people to have rigid boundaries then it is damaging. When religion teaches people to love life then it is salvific. Religions must foster healthy relationships between individuals and groups between humanity and the entire creation.

Now let us look at Jesus. Jesus came announcing life. "I have come so that you have life, and have it in abundance." He promises abundant blessing and unimaginable greenness. Jesus also talks about himself as a vine and source of all fertility. "I am the vine and you are the branches. Whoever remains in me, with me in him, bears fruit in plenty."

In order to be in love with life we must heal the wounds of self- negation. Without self love it is not possible to love others and nature. From eternity human beings are called to their royal personhood. Persons like Jesus, Basavanna, Buddha and Akkamahadevi paid the price for criticising man made monarchies and redefining kingships and redistributing it among all people.

In order to allow ourselves to be healed and to become instruments of healing we must learn the art of "letting go." I do not mean learning to let go merely things and people. I mean the letting go of the attitude of addiction. A compulsive, competitive workaholic culture like ours teaches us to cling to our ego, possessions and power. We must not only let go of these but also religious control, ascetic control, and images of self, others and God. Then we experience the nothingness and stillness. This is not merely emptiness. It is a state of being pregnant with new creation.

The path of letting go gives us insight into the sins of addiction. Letting go increases our receptivity and liberates us helps us to be in love with life. Clinging is ultimately a refusal to grow. Growth facilitates healing. See a rose plant when time is ripe, it is cut and then new branches develop. There is growth and then it blossoms again.

An important aspect of letting go is forgiveness. Forgiveness heals wounds. We are in fact saved by the power of forgiveness. We commit a mistake and then our self-esteem gets lowered in our view of self. We do not want to forgive ourselves because we are attached to an image of self. We do not love ourselves truly as we are. We project an image and then we try to prove it. In this process we get attached to it.

IN ORDER TO LOVE OTHERS FIRST OF ALL
WE MUST LOVE OURSELVES UNCONDITIONALLY.
UNCONDITIONAL LOVE AND UNCONDITIONAL HAPPINESS
GO TOGETHER

Another important aspect of letting go is living a mindful existence. Life is a continuously flowing river. When you cling and do not let go you loose the 'precious eternal NOW'. When you are always in the present- living mindful existence, then you are not only alive every moment, but also you can witness the flow of life.

In order to become instruments of healing we must learn to be comfortable with differences. To let others be different, to be themselves. We are uncomfortable with difference when there is insecurity within us and when there is inner refusal to be ourselves.

We can be effective instruments of healing when we are at home with our deepest self. This is the place where God rests. As Meister Ekhart has put it, "God is at home, it is we who have gone out for a walk."

We do not let others be themselves because we keep on projecting on to others our own attitudes, fears and disappointments. Authentic relating is possible only when we let go these and let others be themselves. When we stop projecting we start relaxing. Letting go of our projections gives the feeling of sinking. This deep sinking within takes us to the inner recesses where God rests. This process helps us to return to our origins, to experience the wholeness again.

Letting go and emptying can be a painful process because of our attachments. In order to let go pain first of all we must embrace it. If we do not let pain be pain then it will haunt us in different ways. Then we will become victims of pain.

When we let pain be pain then we become healers. As Mahatma Gandhi put it, "To make progress we must not make speeches and organize mass meeting but be prepared for mountains of suffering.

Pain is real, there is deep, ineffable pain everywhere. It is not only joy but also pain that links us with one another. All social movements and peoples' organizations were born of shared pain. In our depths we are all interconnected with one another. In the words of Julian of Norwich, "When Christ was in pain we were in pain. All creatures of God's Creation that can suffer pain suffered with him. The sky and the earth failed at the time of Christ's dieing because he too was part of nature."

We must embrace pain so that we might let go of it. Only then we can truly embrace life, embrace love, compassion. Then we become healers.

Exerise : 10 Meditation on Flowing River

Lie down flat on the ground on your back.

Take three deep breaths.

Keep breathing deeply and slowly.

Do relaxation exercise by being aware of each part of your body one after another.

Now visualize yourself as a flowing river. Listen to the sound of the flowing water.

The chemistry of your body keeps on changing every moment, your feelings and thoughts also keep on changing. Every moment you are a new person.

Now let go the past and welcome the present moment

Life is a continuous movement of letting go the past and being in the present.

Letting go the past moment and welcoming the new moment takes place simultaneously.

If you get stuck with the past moment, However painful or pleasant it is then you loose the precious eternal 'NOW'

5

Significance of Meditation in the Pursuit of Happiness

The street cleaner has to take his task of sweeping as the starting point for meditation. So, likewise, must the potter take his task of producing clay utensil on his potter's wheel and the cobbler, his handicrafts. Here, again, therefore, it is evident that one may do what he will so long as he is clearly aware what he is doing. Every activity is of equal value as a basis for a dharana exercise. —*Claudio Naranjo*

WHAT IS MEDITATION ?

Human beings aspire to become, something, 'what we describe as higher than who we think we are' at present, to become the self we are capable of being. In a way this can never happen because we already are the true self we aspire to become. We desire to become higher than who we think we are at present because of our lack of awareness of who we are at present. We are aware of only certain fragments of our self. We intuitively know that we are capable of being the Self consisting of Wholeness.

What we do not know is that we already are Whole. Our ego is formed in the process of interacting with the physical world around us and our mind gets conditioned to believe what it sees and what seems to be logical. Hence the consciousness that we have is merely an acquired consciousness due to collecting information in the process of interacting with the world. The acquired consciousness does not know who we are because this consciousness is clouded due to the unconscious identification of the ego with mental states, moods, sensations and objective perceptions, which keep on changing. Self and God are also unconsciously identified with these changing circumstances, mental states and moods. In this state the person only gets more and more confused not knowing who and what one is. In this viewpoint the more one tries to understand one self the more illusions one builds the more you struggle with your moods and mental states the more you get attached to the sensory perceptions. It seems as if we are passing through a dark tunnel of ignorance. As long as this ignorance persists we will be living an illusionary world.

The realization of our true nature is commonly believed to be too difficult to achieve. Generally people believe that self- realization is meant only for saints and exceptional people and not for common people.

This is because of the illusion created due to our psycho-physical existence. At the psycho-physical level our consciousness is limited to acquired consciousness. The acquired consciousness has illusional concepts and emotional states which block clear awareness. Even though at the soul level we are inclined to transcendental awakening and we can sense and know who we are, we are conditioned to believe in our limitation at the physical level.

We get to know ourselves intuitively as if looking through a dark glass dimly. When we start trusting our intuition and proceed in the path we are able to see ourselves directly and clearly. This is possible when we let go our acquired consciousness and overcome the conditioned part of ourselves.

There is an innate urge in us to know who we are and to free ourselves from the ignorance and illusions.

This innate urge guides our actions and pushes us into a path, this path ultimately is ourselves. Through this path we take different forms. In fact we become the path in order to discover ourselves to move from darkness to light, ignorance to awareness and from unhappiness to happiness. In this path we learn to know ourselves. First of all we have to learn not to identify ourselves with mental states and moods and environmental conditions and other circumstances in which we exist. We have to learn to remove our attention from the changing and temporary conditions, moods and mental states and fix the attention on to our inner real nature. When we know that we are not our circumstances, bodies, or minds, we are provided an opportunity to free ourselves from being overtly influenced by them. That is we will not cling to the conditioning and will not take refuge in the security of acquired consciousness. Initially it may be like as if the ground on which we stand is collapsing but by doing so we are opened up to the higher realities. As stated by Davis (1994 : 26), "Preliminary meditation processes work directly with this fundamental problem of outer identification that blinds us to the truth of ourselves and to perceptions of higher realities. From the beginning of practice, the meditator learns to sit still and internalize attention, causing awareness to withdraw from sense organs and mental transformations and turn back on itself. It is only when internalized attention flows without disturbance to the chosen focus of concentration or transcendental possibilities that meditation actually occurs."

The process of letting go and withdrawing our attention from our bodies and senses is like crossing a bridge and making a connection to the other side. The word 'meditation,' then actually means to attend. To meditate, one has to learn to attend to something with full devotion and commitment. One has to train the mind in order to cultivate attention. Only by training the mind one can begin to systematically understand the whole process of the inward journey. Together with this one has to learn to be still physically, to have a serene breath and a calm mind.

The internalization of attention flowing without disturbance means already connecting to higher realities.

Without establishing this possibility of connecting to higher realities while having its physical existence we can never really know who we really are. That is why meditation plays fundamentally an important role in the discovery of who we are. Meditation is an experiential path. Meditation is one of the paths that puts a person in touch with higher realities. It puts us in touch with ourselves.

In meditation awareness is focused inwardly. This focussing of attention follows a systematic path from the most external parts of one's personality, that is the body and senses, to the innermost, the mind itself. In order to be familiar with this path, one must tread this path regularly, then the mind gets calmed and purified. It is important to know one's mind systematically in order to calm its disturbances. The human mind is like a body of water. The jewel of consciousness is at the bottom of this water. By calming the mind one can know and reach this jewel of consciousness, the highest goal of life.

When we find the jewel of consciousness we will know our true self. Until we find our true self we cannot be happy because till then we will know only bits and pieces of self. These bits and pieces are the fragments and we mistake them for our whole real self in its earthly abode. Because each fragment acts like an individual ego, we become victims of conflicts between different egos'. Then we feel torn between the desires of various fragments. Naturally when we function from the fragments of our self then there is imbalance in our life. When we initiate action from imbalace it causes more imbalance.

When we find ourselves with full soul consciousness we will get back our wholeness. As we progress along the path the unfoldment of the soul takes place and we ultimately get to know the self what we long desired to become. In the present moment we do know that in fact we already are that what we desire to become but as the unfoldment of soul progresses we move closer and closer and then ultimately become one with IT. Ultimately when we are one with IT we will know that we have always been that.

The essence of the method of meditation is to learn to observe objectively whatever comes into the mind by being mindful. To do that, the mind needs an object of concentration and an inner point of focus. The mental object for concentration is called a 'mantra'. The 'mantra' is given by the spiritual teacher, based on whatever is appropriate to the personality of the aspirant in her/his stage of development. The 'mantra' guides the aspirant on the inner journey.

CAUSES FOR STRESS

The present mode of living of most of the general population is competitive. Competition rather than cooperation is the rule of the game. Cooperation exists mostly when there is self gain. Relationships are also based on what one gets from the other. Love and happiness are also searched outside of oneself. People fall in love in order to get love, to feel loved and to be loved. An individual living in our society gets message that she/he somehow should be better than the other. So people keep on entering into a competitive life style created and maintained in our society by people who are trying to prove that they are better and more successful than the other.

The modern way of life generates fear and anxiety about ones life and distrust about the other. This way of living generates insecurity. When a person is insecure he or she finds it even more difficult to live harmoniously with oneself, nature and others. In this state of existence there are greater possibilities to feel dissatisfied no matter what a person is doing. People in this state also find it difficult to live one's life as one would like it to be instead keep on trying to be acceptable to people with whom she/he interacts even without knowing what is acceptable to the other person. This in effect generates more dissatisfaction and insecurity. Thus one gets caught up into a vicious circle.

The way we are guided by competition shows that we are in complete oblivion of who we are. So people do not actually care what happens to the other as long as their needs are met. Hence the world around us including other people are used as objects of our satisfaction or dissatisfaction. The 'ego' of a person becomes the center of everything. It is also falsely mistaken for the real self. Most of our interactions and our economies are guided by this ego.

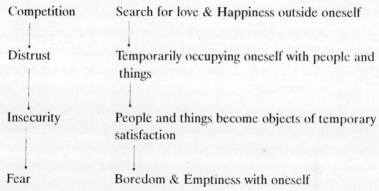

Competition	Search for love & Happiness outside oneself
Distrust	Temporarily occupying oneself with people and things
Insecurity	People and things become objects of temporary satisfaction
Fear	Boredom & Emptiness with oneself

Unhappiness

People find their lives caught up in this vicious circle but feel helpless without knowing what to do. The illusion is created by the beliefs they hold and these beliefs are absorbed from the society where one lives. As a result people's lives are controlled by outside forces. This in fact generates even more insecurity so people try to please others and follow whatever is considered trendy in society. This drives a person to hoard and achieve more and more material gains and look for positions which make a person feel powerful over the other. Thus our society creates people who seem to be powerful and who control others yet afraid to be alone and experience boredom with oneself. People then become shallow, they make a lot of noise but it becomes only empty sound.

The modern way of life leads people to materialistic viewpoint and human beings are intoxicated by it. We are deceived by the senses and constantly drink through the senses. It also makes people workaholics. It makes people think that the more they have the greater they become. There is no end to this. It takes away the joy from peoples lives. How much should a person possess to feel wealthy ? One has to stop and answer this question. To answer this question one must first of all recognise and identify the addictions in one's life.

This way of living subjects a person to a lot of stress and strain and takes a person away from oneself. The more a person moves away from ones real self the more unhappy she or he becomes.

The more one moves away from one's true self, the false self takes over. The false self is guided by the outside forces because it learns what is right and wrong from the society in which one lives. It learns what kind of clothes one should wear and in what kind of house one should live in. It collects lot of information and also learns skills for surviving in a society where constantly one has to take care of oneself and know how to behave. This false self has acquired consciousness. This consciousness is acquired from the community or society where one lives and interacts. When one is in touch with ones true self then one intuitively knows what one wants, what one must speak and how one must act, one does it spontaneously with precision and without any fear.

All human beings search for happiness and contentment of the soul. Most of us look for it outside of ourselves. We may even try hard to find it but when we look for it outside pretty soon we feel bored and unhappy. Human beings can never find ultimate happiness outside oneself because happiness is a internal state. The outside objects can help a person temporarily to escape from boredom and unhappiness. They help you for the time being to divert your attention and then once again you start feeling empty and sad.

Contentment of the Soul and happiness keep on elluding you like a mirage, you keep on running after it and do not find it.

Ultimately what a person really looks for is happiness. Search for happiness is innate in every human being. It is part of the nature of every soul even then we do not find it because of our acquired consciousness. In todays society the average human being has the awareness of acquired consciousness only. Generally the average human being is not in touch with the inner core or the actual reality of who he or she is, which is residing deep inside. What we are in touch with is the outer layer, the acquired consciousness. This acquired consciousness keeps on changing depending on our thoughts, beliefs, and the information which we keep on acquiring. Thus the mood of the person also keeps on changing since our feelings to a large extent depend on what we think. This in turn create chemical changes in our body.

If our own thoughts determine our emotions and actions, then we must realise that actually we are the masters of our destiny. At present we do not know this truth. This is because we do not know who we are and we are not in touch with our whole 'True Self'. We are only in touch with the fragments of the Self. One must first of all have a genuine desire to find the True Self, and to know the purpose of life. And then if one truly searches one can be in touch with one's True Self, also know the purpose of life and live a fulfilled life. Some people do think that some unseen God is responsible for all the misery in their life. In reality we are the designers of our life and we are responsible for the kind of patterns we design in our life. We in fact create our own path. The more we become aware of our Self, the more we will realise that we are creating our own life and also the circumstances in which we live but right now we only have a limited vision of our life, hence we are not seeing the whole.

Just like a person cannot put her foot twice in the same water in a flowing river so also a human being is not the same from moment to moment. We keep on changing. This is because of the nature of our mind. Happiness can be found only inside and not outside of one's true self. The primary and the only source of real fulfillment of life lies within us. This is because our real self exists in wholesome purity at the innermost level of Being. Here is the pure bliss, undisturbed peace, happiness and flawless knowledge. It is untouched by mundane conditions and transitory events. Hence the final solution for all problems also lies within us.

That is why the secret of happiness seems to be lying hidden within the secret of being in touch with ones true self. There is an innate urge within every human soul to have awareness restored to its actual Being, where there is undisturbed wholeness.

Meditation helps us to get in touch with our real nature and to know who we are. Meditation is a path towards self-realization and illumination of consciousness. Self-realization is conscious awareness of ourselves as spiritual beings. This conscious awareness is demonstrated through our awakened soul consciousness and healthy, creatively functional lives. The full illumination of consciousness removes illusions and frees the Spirit. When there is self-realization and illumination of consciousness, the acquired consciousness dissolves and the Spirit becomes free from darkness. IT awakens ITSELF to unending light.

GOALS OF MEDITATION

Human beings have an innate urge to be the higher self. This would mean to be whole, to share love and be happy with one self, one another, and whole creation. This includes being able to manage relationships with self and others lovingly, selflessly and skillfully. This would also mean using ones capacities to be co-creators with God. Love has been travelling for eternity. Human beings are travelling on this path to reach the final goal where transitoriness of sense and changes do not effect them.

The present perspective of living to which one is exposed to, subjects a person to a lot of stress and incapacitates him or her from getting in touch with the inner person. This in fact prevents the person from knowing the real purpose of ones life. Functioning from imbalance creates more imbalance and people do not find fulfillment in their lives. Unfulfillment generates more and more possibilities for unhappiness and selfish relationships.

The inner growth of the person has a relationship to his/her outer action and that is why the inner growth of a person has an impact on the quality of relationships one cultivates. Inner growth does not mean separating oneself from the society and living in the forest and on mountains. The inner journey of the person is reflected in the outer actions and way of life of the person. The task of being enlightened is accomplished in the world and not outside the world.

If one discovers oneself and knows who he or she is then the person not only frees himself or herself from the impact of the perspective which makes a person perceive oneself as an isolated entity but also frees oneself from the present way of living of our society which incapacitates from nurturing loving relationships that are life giving. Then people become capable of finding an alternative way of living.

Having a conscious desire to be happy and getting in touch with oneself is the first step towards discovering who one actually is. If one has really examined the body, its needs, wants and desires then you see only one reality.

Meditation awakens us to the reality of who we are and helps us to be free from the conditioning of the mind. Though the ultimate goal of meditation is union with God, there are many side effects of meditation.

A person practicing meditation becomes calm, peaceful gains the capacity for better concentration. He or she is able to have a positive impact on the surroundings through positive energy. A person starts managing even the economic life better then before. On the whole the person begins to enjoy an improved quality of life by managing the affairs of the world more effectively and efficiently.

The goal of meditation is the fusion of the individual with the universal. This would mean attainment of liberation while living. In Indian life this is considered to be the highest experience. A human being is considered to be a spark of the cosmos, the microcosm parallels everything in the microcosm. As stated by Mookerjee (1982), 'according to tantric principles, all that exists in the universe must also exist in the individual body. If we can analyse one human being, we shall be able to analyse the entire universe, because it is believed that all is built on the same plane. The purpose is to search for the whole truth within, so that one may realize one's inner self, unfolding the basic reality of the universe.'

The goal of Eastern Meditation is self-realization and not the achievement of pleasant mood or successful living. The goal of Eastern Meditation practices can be summed up as being in union with the Absolute or God. The goal of Western meditation as given by Masters (1989), "to achieve improvement in one's outer self." In the Western meditation practice 'a positive self- improvement statement' with a Spiritual reference is used for meditation. However as a person progresses in the path of self- realization, *i.e.,* as a person moves closer and closer to the real self there are visible changes in the person in terms of the kind of energy one exuberates. Practice of meditation helps to gain relaxation, renew one's energy factor and in certain instances to heal physical ailments. Person becomes happier and more efficient in functioning than before.

Happiness and successful living are surface benefits and outer signs of the inner grace received by the person. Generally the way of living for most of the people is stressful in today's world. Hence there is an ever growing need for people to learn the practice of meditation, if even just for its surface benefits.

Davis (1994 : 23) is of the opinion that, "More immediate indications of awakened spiritual consciousness are the spontaneous manifestations of radiant calmness, mental clarity, spontaneity, simplicity, and natural ease in relating to circumstances."

Beginning a process to get in touch with oneself is of utmost importance for spiritual awakening. This path then leads to Self- realization. Self-realization is not difficult to achieve. When right understanding and right endeavor are coordinated it is easy to experience Self-realization.

One can get in touch with the 'True Self' with the help of meditation. Getting in touch with one's True Self is possible only through spiritual awakening. And as stated by Rama (1988), "There is no other way to spiritual awakening except through meditation, intense devotion, and right action." The spiritual awakening is done through the help of kundalini can be conscious or unconscious. One can consciously awaken the kundalini force. In the modern language it is called 'the unconscious' and in the traditional language it is the kundalini shakti. When this 'shakti' is awakened you become creative, insightful and also energetic. The shakti when it is awakened from its dormant state and from its latent state to active state the spiritual transformation of the personality takes place.

When meditational practice is combined with intentional living one can actualize the beneficial results for day to day living almost immediately. Because of the stress one is subjected to many people do not get the rest they need when they sleep. As a result they suffer from low energy reserves, irritability, poor concentration, inefficiency in performance at work, lower resistance to disease or psycho-physical ailments.

When one practices meditation breathing becomes slower and the person enjoys mental tranquility. This provides the meditator deep conscious rest and renews the whole person giving more rest than what one usually gets during sleep. Even when the person is not interested in spiritual growth meditation practiced once or twice a day for twenty or thirty minutes has beneficial results.

Benson (1976) studied the practitioners of Transcendental Meditation and found out the relaxation response to meditation. The main physiological features of the response are as follows :

"The heart rate of meditators decreases by, on average, about three beats per minute. The rate of breathing decreases.

The body's consumption of oxygen decreases, by as much as twenty percent. There is a marked decrease in the body's rate of metabolism.

Blood lactate decreases. Lactate is a substance produced by the metabolism of the skeletal muscles. High levels of lactate in the blood are associated with attacks of anxiety. Blood pressure is at normal levels. It was found that meditation reduces blood pressure in individuals who have high blood pressure before starting meditation.

The brain produces alpha and perhaps theta waves-alpha waves are slower and linked with states of relaxation; theta waves are slower still." The findings definitely show that because of deep relaxation and the physiological and psychological changes that occur during meditation, physical tension and mental anxiety fade as stress is reduced.

One of the common illnesses today is hypertension. It is closely connected with people's way of living.

Its debilitating effects are like-killing since it interferes with the normal functioning of physical systems. Its symptoms are generally high blood pressure, migraine headaches and inappropriate anger. When a person practices meditation regularly these symptoms vanish. This is because when a person has practiced meditation for some months mind becomes more stable and the capacity to cope with stressful situation has been enhanced. It is a common experience among the meditators that they need less sleep and are awakened more refreshed. Physically the body feels lighter, the muscles have 'let go' from tension and they experience buoyancy, specially soon after meditation.

Davis (1994 : 35) reports that, "Contemplative meditation that results in sustained superconscious episodes regulates biochemical secretions and infuses the body with superior energy-frequencies which spiritualize it. Long-term meditators tend to experience a diminishment of biological aging processes. They have higher energy levels, keen interest in living, faster and stronger immune systems than the persons who are not long-term meditators. Their biological ages are several years younger than their calendar years."

A self-realized person is completely conscious and the effects of their personal presence upon others are morally and spiritually elevating. This is because of the inner energy and light that is radiated and channelized out through the person to the surroundings.

During meditation there is expansion of the consciousness of a person. Since ancient times the practitioners of meditation have discovered that the expansion of consciousness and thus getting in touch with the reality is facilitated by the arousal of the primal energy which lies dormant at the bottom of the spine. This energy is called 'Kundalini.' The Kundalini can be awakened through the practice of kundalini-yoga. The object of the tantric practice of kundalini-Yoga is to awaken this cosmic energy and cause it to unite with Siva, the Pure Consciousness pervading the whole universe.

The preparations to awaken the kundalini are more important than the awakening of the kundalini itself.

One must genuinely purify ones mind and clarify the purpose of life. The awakening of the kundalini shakti would mean activating a great latent power, which is lying dormant in oneself. If it is activated without proper preparation it can be deeply disturbing and disorienting to the person. That is why uncompromising honesty with oneself is utmost important.

One must prepare oneself to meditate honestly. Whatever the desires one has, they are strengthened during meditation. Hence first of all one must empty oneself of all the desires. There should be only one desire to go deep within oneself, i.e., the desire for meditation. The desires are strengthend because of the expansion of mind. In meditation one becomes aware of the deeper levels of one's being, there is an expansion of consciousness.

The kundalini shakti is awakened in two stages. During the first stage one uses certain techniques and simply awakens the kundalini. During the second stage one learns to lead it. To actually awaken the kundalini energy through yogic methods for the upward journey along the

Brahma-nadi, the practitioner must summon all the strength and skill at his or her command. The practitioner first of all must take up the posture that is suitable and in which one feels comfortable. You can sit crossed legged on the ground, on a carpet or a cushion or you can also sit on a chair. The back should be straight. One must sit in stillness during the time of meditation. The initiation of the process by which Kundalini is aroused is done through 'sense withdrawal' and by directing the will-power to the vital air that is inhaled and held in Pranayama, guiding its circulatory movement through Ida and Pingala down to the base of the spine into the space where Kundalini lies coiled.

The power of meditative practices is reinforced by the pranayama done for the arousal of Kundalini energy.

Breath provides the means of symbiosis between different forms of life and also between existence and awareness. Yoga is concerned to direct this bio-motor force towards the expansion of consciousness in the human organism. It is through the science of breathing that the body's subtle centers are vitalized. The devotion for the practice of meditation is also important. That is why it is necessary to fix a time during the day either morning or evening or twice a day for the practice of meditation.

In my experience I have found that when meditation is practiced concentration is effortless. The nature of this meditation may be described as effortless attention' or 'effortless awareness.' Hewitt (1992) reports that in the meditation training centres in Burma and Thailand, monks and lay persons practicing sitting meditation and mobile meditation through most of the day find concentration effortless. This in fact helps a person to be more at ease with oneself and the universe, leads to easier personal relationships.

I have observed in my experience of meditation that the practice of meditation effects changes in the quality and quantity of energy at psycho-spiritual and physical levels. In fact there is a change in the psycho-biological health of the person. Psychosomatic ailments are cured. The biological organism enjoys renewed physical strength and health. The person begins to experience a certain lightness in the body. Body feels younger than before. There is an increased confidence to do better in the management of day to day life.

This includes the management of relationships as well as the area of job or economic life of the person. There is increased creativity in all the outer expressions of life. This increased creativity is visible in personal life as well as in the management of economic achievements of the person. It helps the person to be more successful. There is more love in one's life, towards one self, to those to whom the practitioner relates and to all life and creation. Person becomes more sensitive and loving. It is as if the person has become more intelligent than before.

The practitioner of Meditation becomes more aware of the existence of one reality and the eternal existence of ones wholeness and the wholeness of this one reality. This in fact helps the person to relate with oneself, other people and whole creation in a sensitive, sensible, intelligent and loving manner. The inner realization is expressed in the outer actions of the person.

In fact it has been discovered that people feel more secure and relaxed in the presence of a praciitoner whose soul consciousness is awakened. This is because of the life giving quality of the primal energy and the expanded consciousness of the person. This energy has the quality of healing and renewing life. As the person goes deeper and deeper into meditation he or she also gains more insights into wholesome living. This includes the kind of food one may eat or the exercises one must practice. It brings about a change in the way of living of the person.

As an interim step between present way of living and finding the true Self, it is also important to learn to deal with Stress.

It is possible to reduce Stress by practicing certain techniques. Benson (1976) found that it was possible to elicit "an integrated response opposite to the fight-or-flight response." This response is not unique to eastern Transcendental Meditation. Indeed lowered oxygen consumption, heart rate, respiration, and blood lactate are indicative of decreased activity of the sympathetic nervous system and represent a hypometabolic or restful state. On the other hand, the physiological changes of the fight-or-flight response are associated with increased sympathetic nervous system activity and represent a hypermetablic state.

The physiological changes observed during Relaxation Response can also be elicited by certain western techniques relaxation such as autogenic training, progressive relaxation and hypnosis. The advantage of Transcendental Meditation over these western techniques is that meditation usually is practised by oneself, whereas the western techniques, specially in their earlier stages require an instructor. Besides meditation is a path towards self- realization. Relaxation is only a side effect of the practice and not the goal as in western relaxation techniques.

There has been a great deal of research into the physiological and psychological changes among people who practice Transcendental Meditation. It has been found that Meditation helps people break addictions, become more efficient, cope well with stress and move in the direction of becoming more spontaneous and fulfilled joyous living. People who practice Meditation also show greater progress towards self-actualisation.

According to Maslow (1962), self-actualising people represent the psychgologically most healthy people in society. Self-actualising people have 'B' — being — values and 'peak experiences'. 'B' values include wholeness, effortlessness truth, and honesty. And 'peak experiences' are marked by 'total attention' perceiving 'the whole of being', ego transcendence' and other hallmarks of mystical consciousness. Among the clients who came to me with symptoms of hypertension, not being able to concentrate on work and increased irritability and sleeplessness, those who practiced meditation showed improvement with in a weeks time. Almost with in 15 days they had achieved mental calmeness and increased efficiency at work.

There was an improvement in the quality of their sleep. They were able to love more and quality of their relationships improved. When you practice meditation living seems to flow effortlessly and at the same time it also becomes more joyous and fulfilling though you do not do meditation to elevate mood.

As reported by Benson (1976) "an examination of blood lactate levels before and after meditation often reveals a reduction of blood lactate levels, which are usually higher when one is in a 'fight or flight" psycho-physical state. This is a common condition for many people who feel it necessary to struggle to survive or who perceive threats to their well-being from real or imagined sources.

Levy and Monte (1997), have reported that "Researchers at the University of Miami Medical School have found that daily meditation increases immune-cell activity. A 10 to 20 minute session per day lowers blood pressure, slows the heart rate, relaxes muscles and creates a more balanced hormonal condition."

DISCUSSION

The goal of meditation is union with God or the union of the individual with the universal. However the practitioners of meditation through ancient times have found that meditation improves physical and mental health mainly by reducing stress. Scientists have done research and found that there are physiological and psychological changes produced by the practice of meditation. Meditation elicits a 'Relaxation Response' this is the opposite of the fight-or-flight response to danger. Benson's (1976) study of practitioners of Transcendental Meditation, in fact has proved the benefits received by the body through the practice of meditation. Hence one can confidently say that the regular practice of meditation definitely helps a person to cure hypertension and psychosomatic ailments.

The rest and relaxation gained through meditation are in many ways superior to sleep. Meditation practiced twice a day, once in the morning and once in the evening for about 20 minutes duration leads to improvements not only in physical health but also clarity of mind and equanimity. Actually the techniques of meditation were devised for spiritual and mystical purposes, the improvements in pyscho-physical health are side benefits of meditation. Even if one does meditation only for the purpose of these side benefits then it is worth practicing meditition. Generally people are not aware of these side benefits. People have a misconception that only those who are not interested in the world and those who want to isolate themselves from the world practice meditation.

There is meaning and purpose for the existence of human beings in this world. Human beings consciously or unconsciously keep on searching for the meaning and purpose of existence. The actual purpose of life becomes apparent to people only when they are in touch with themselves. The present way of living in society takes a person away from oneself and makes him or her perceive that they are separate and isolated entities from other human beings and other life. The more a person goes away from one's real self the more one is subjected to stress. Thus people get into a vicious circle of becoming more and more unhappy. Hence there is an urgent need for people to get in touch with the real self. Meditation helps people to get in touch with themselves. It also helps people to free themselves from the conditioning of mind.

As reported by Rama (1988) and Mookerjee (1995) there are specific techniques of breathing which help the upward movement of the primal energy, Kundalini. This in fact strengthens the practice of meditation. Every human being searches happiness, peace and love in the world, in day to day living because there is wholeness in the inner core of person. Humanity as a whole has not yet achieved this consciousness which would help them to know who they are and to experience the wholeness within.

A person living in the present day society undergoes a lot of stress. This is due to the perspective of living to which one is subjected to. A person born in this society internalises certain beliefs, prevalent in society and learns to view life accordingly. As a result an individual living in the society perceives oneself as an isolated entity separated from the rest of people and the whole creation. It is highly important for modern men and women to find an alternative perspective which helps them to get in touch with their true Self.

Meditation helps people to achieve expansion of consciousness and to get in touch with reality. It also helps the person to be free from the conditioning of the mind. The actual goal of meditation is union with God.

It has been observed that among the practitioners of meditation there are certain visible changes in terms the kind of energy one exuberates. The person starts enjoying better psycho-physical and spiritual health than before. There is increased confidence in the person and starts performing better in personal and professional life. The inner realization becomes visible in the outer expressions of the person. The person becomes more loving. Person also changes his or her life style into a more wholesome way of living.

The side benefits itself of meditation are so great that it is worth practicing. This in fact could attract people to practice meditation and then eventually may help to know who they are and to discover the purpose of life.

6

Human Process Lab Reports

Three Human process lab reports are presented here.

These workshops were designed according to the requests made by the organisations and companies. They were also designed based on the needs of the participants.

Most of the sessions were partially structured and some of the sessions were unstructured. This method was worked out in order to help the participants to explore themselves and achieve the growth they wanted to achieve and simultaneously to meet the demand of the agency.

Only the gist and main points are presented. The detailed personal sharing by the participants as well as the details of the dynamics are not presented here. We have mainly focused on the insights derived by the participants and some of the exercises of the lab.

This kind of workshops are different for different groups since they are also based on the level of growth of the participants. Every participant can begin only from where they are.

HUMAN PROCESS LAB : I
SELF AWARENESS

Human beings have a tendency to form habits and most of us are driven by habits, which may not always respond to the needs of our body precisely. The cells of our body are alive and they know what they need. You can raise the level of awareness of your by listening to it. You can gain major benefits by using the power of body awareness in your day today life.

Session : 1 Body Awareness

Part : (i)

Lie down or sit comfortably with your eyes closed.

Take three deep breaths. While breathing let the air go through your nostrils, chest, stomach and the abdomen, while breathing out let go even the last bit of air from the abdomen.

Now keep breathing deeply and slowly.

Start paying attention to each part of your body starting from the toes and then gradually moving to the top of your body to the head

Let your attention linger on each part in a relaxed manner. Do not rush either while tensing or while relaxing the body parts.

Tense the left foot then relax,

tense the left leg then relax,

now right foot : tense-relax,

right leg : tense-relax,

right buttock : tense-relax,

left buttock : tense-relax,

lower back : tense relax,

upper back : tense-relax,

abdomen : tense-relax,

stomach : tense-relax,

chest : tense-relax,

shoulders : tense-relax

neck : tense-relax

face : tense-relax

brow : tense-relax

forehead : tense-relax

Now your whole body is relaxed.

Increase this relaxation by focused intention.

Allow your body to feel light.

Part : (ii) Attention is Healing

Now be aware of uncomfortable sense in your body if any,

Be with the uncomfortable sense or be with the body part which has pain or any kind of ache, embrace the pain, or ache or the uncomfortable sense and dialogue with the part of the body which has the uncomfortable sense, or pain or ache.

Awareness, focused attention and intention help us to regain the balance of our body and mind. Most of the time most of us are driven by the ambitions of our 'ego'. We get caught up in the pursuit of money, career, wealth and self-importance. When we are so driven by our ego, we drift further and further away from our actual self. The exercise on body awareness helps us to transcend our ego and listen to our body, which in turn is a doorway to get in touch with our spirit, *i.e.,* our actual self. Awareness and intentions are body-mind centered. Ego not only drives us away from our true self it also blocks us from reaching out to self. It acts as many layers of veil that hides and prevents us from accessing the inner wisdom and light and keeps us in darkness.

During the exercise it is important to learn not **to** struggle with the ego, be friendly with the ego and ask it **to** cooperate and participate in the exercise.

Session 2 : Becoming Aware of ones Beliefs

Resource person facilitated to enter into a meditative mood.

Recall one belief that you learnt from each of the following institutions, which still form the part of your belief system :

> your family,
> your school,
> church or devotion circle and
> friends circle.

Each belief has both positive and negative aspects. So there is a need to look at them critically. Beliefs are alive and not dead. Beliefs are powerful. Beliefs have formed us. Our "being" is influenced by family, friends, culture and church etc. We are a bundles of beliefs. When we are aware of our beliefs, then we need not struggle within. We can see the beliefs in various forms in the our relationship with self, others, nature and God or the higher power that we experience. So when we are aware of our beliefs, bits of various shapes of energy within are reorganised and we can bring about a positive change. Beliefs are made and beliefs make a human being. Animals have their natural characters but human beings do not and have the capacity to become what he wants because human nature is energy.

Session : 3 Learning to be Comfortable with the Self

Participants were asked to go for a brisk walk for 20 minutes. After the walk light physical exercise was done.

Participants were then asked to take few deep breaths. After this keep breathing deeply and slowly.

Close your eyes.

Imagine the body to be another person and have a dialogue.

Write the dialogue.

Concentrate on any part of your body.

Have the dialogue with that part.

Sharing with others.

Session : 4 Self-Acceptance

Resource person facilitated the process to help the participants to enter into a meditative mood.

Asked the participants to visualize the following fantasy :

Lie down or take a comfortable position and close your eyes.

Imagine going out of the room towards woods.

Now you are crossing a river and going up the mountain.

You see another mountain and a rock.

The rock resembles your face. See it properly.

Few chiseling instruments are also lying by.

Would you like to make any changes using those chiselers ?

Do it if you want.

You will be given 20 minutes.

Insights :

Many of the participants did not like some or other part of their face. Some felt ashamed of their colour. This is due to the internalised concepts about beauty and about the understanding on white skin as more superior than dark skin. It is interesting to gain insights as to how the concepts about beauty and skin colour effect our self understanding, performance and achievements in life.

The prevalent beliefs about 'what kind of a body is beautiful,' are internalised by the people. This understanding not only effects their own performance but also the way they look at others, the relations that are built up and the way the other is assessed. Little do we think that these are only concepts formulated by someone according to her or his convenience. As the saying goes 'beauty lies in beholders eyes.' Beauty does lie in the perceivers eyes. It depends on how the perceiver is conditioned to perceive beauty.

The whole creation including human beings are neither beautiful nor ugly. They just are. Now we can make it beautiful or ugly.

The dominant groups who impose their culture on others and determine the cultural trends of the main stream also impose the concepts of beauty. When you accept these concepts of beauty your view gets limited, then you can not see beauty elsewhere. These concepts are not absolute, it is an illusion created by the concepts, which temporarily look like reality. When the concepts change then new illusions are created.

WHEN YOU DECONDITION YOURSELF
FROM THESE PREVALENT CONCEPTS
YOU CAN PERCEIVE BEAUTY IN YOURSELF
AND EVERYWHERE.
USE YOUR POWER TO CREATE YOUR REALITY

Session : 5 Create Your Own Reality

I step : Music is on.

Dance to the tune of the Music.

Create your own dance, dance of life.

Keep flowing to the tune of music,

Do not just repeat the steps of dance that you have learnt.

Create your own steps.

Listen to the music, then listen to your body, see what movements your body wants to make. How does it want to flow ?

Dance. Make bigger movements.

Now take a partner and create your own dance.

Reflection on the following :

* How the body is conditioned to move and carry itself in a certain way.

* You can experience larger flow of energy within yourself when you free yourself from this conditioning.

Some participations were uncomfortable to dance alone. They felt better to dance with a partner. Reflection on :

* What happens when you are alone ?

* Why do you feel afraid when you are alone ?

* Why do you believe in "I am weak"

* Why do you call yourself weak when you do not know who you are ?

* Do you know yourself ? Who are you ?

* Are you, your feelings or thoughts or beliefs ?

Some did not dance. Reflect on :

* When you had an opportunity to create your own reality why did not make use of the opportunity. Why are you just satisfied existing in the reality created by others ?

Some are feeling fearful, sad and happy. Some others have a sense that are superior to others and there are others who feel inferior. But self is not our feelings. Feelings come from beliefs. You change your beliefs then you can change your feelings. These beliefs are part of our acquired self. We are good in creating stories, we also like it so we keep on creating certain myths for self and others to believe. In order to create what we want, we want others also to believe the stories that are created by us.

God never wants us to be sad or weak, so do not blame God when you feel sad. God has given us the power to be happy when you want to be happy. So when you are sad just examine the significant beliefs, you are holding, in connection with the present situation. Then ask yourself why are you holding these beliefs ?

Session : 6 Focusing on Purpose of Life

Think that your life has just begun and the life span in one hour.

You are provided with clay, plastic sheets and yourself.

There is neither past not future.

Create whatever you want.

During the sharing the facilitator asked the following questions. Questions depended on the content of sharing by the individual participant.

Questions for reflection.

* Are you satisfied with what you have created ?
* Did you make the best use of the opportunity to live fully ?
* What did you create and why ?
* What do you feel and think about yourself ?
* Why do you want to be great infront of others in the world ?
* Why do you consider yourself greater than others ?
* When you are not greater than others, why do you feel sad ?
* Why do you consider yourself inferior to others ?

Session : 7 Letting Go "Crystal River and Creatures"

The resource person facilitated a process to help the participants to be in a meditative state. Then the exercise on visualisation was presented.

Sit in a comfortable position and close your eyes.

Visualise a stream of flowing water. Several creatures are inside and this is their world. There is strong current on the surface. The creatures are scared and they are clinging to the bottom. One creature tries to come above the water level and looks outside and scared and clings itself to the bottom of the stream. Many try to go to the surface but dare not to come out of the water. But one small creature succeeds in doing so and feels great and says there is much more outside their small world.

The whole exercise was meant to let go the beliefs and not to cling to them and to go ahead and face the situation and discover new things in life.

Reflection on :

To what bottom are you clinging ?

What would mean to you, 'letting go,' of this bottom ?

What are your fears ?

What do you want to do about it ?

Session : 8 Awareness about Relationships

The facilitator helped the participants to enter into a meditative mood.

Sit in a comfortable position and close your eyes.

Take few deep breaths.

Keep breathing deeply and slowly.

Let the faces of significant persons in your life float into your mind.

Just be with them for a while, note what does it really mean to be with them.

Is it a pleasant life giving experience ? If not what else is it ?

How important are these relationships in your life ?

What functions do they fulfill ?

Now let the relationships which you consider as unpleasant come to your mind.

What is unpleasant about these relationships ?

Now let the faces of persons whom you do not trust float into your mind.

Note why you do not trust them.

Now let the faces of people which you consider as life giving float into your mind.

What is life giving in your relationship with them ?

Write down on a sheet of paper the insights derived from the exercise.

Remember whatever you are writing is written for yourself. So be honest with yourself.

Insights :

The expectations from one another in the relationship created hurt feelings. Many had also considered that others were responsible to make them happy and significant people in their life, were responsible for their unhappiness. It was clarified that each one is responsible for ones own happiness. Other people do not have the power to make you happy or sad unless you give them the power to do so.

Questions for reflections :

Why do you believe that when you curse somebody, God also does according to your will ?

Why do you make others responsible for your happiness ?

Why don't you trust yourself ?

Who is responsible for your happiness ?

Words are important and words have power. They come back to us at one point or the other. If we wish good things to happen, these words will come back bringing happiness. If we wish painful things to happen, they will come back creating sorrow and pain. So create and choose your reality.

We are energy. We can create new reality. Experiences are created by each one of us. So one can create any experiences painful or joy. Every one has the power to grow. Events are a means for growth. There is enough power within to bring change within one self. It brings peace and inner joy.

Session : 9   Gaining Confidence to Trust Self and be Transparent with Others

The facilitator challenged the participants with regard to how much they want to stretch themselves. Stretchig self would mean having more energy for self.

Do you share your secrets with others ?

Now you share your secret which you never have shared with any body else.

Sharing from the participants.

HUMAN PROCESS LAB : 2
OPTIONAL RESOURCEFULNESS

Aim   :   Synthesising the Vision of Development and Self Transformation.

Participants   :   16 Managers

Objectives :

* To clarify the vision of personal growth and its relation to achievements in ones life.
* To enable the participants to realise their potential.
* To get in touch with the creativity.
* To develop new vision of development and relationships.
* To view work as creation.

In the Human Process Lab, all the participants were put at ease both physically and mentally. Importance was given to how to enjoy creativity and to be resourceful in achieving meaningful results in one's personal and professional life.

Session on Body Language :

Both verbal and non-verbal communications play a vital role in one's life. Most of the times, less attention is paid to non verbal communication and the important clues given by the body about ones needs and the present psycho-physiological state, which includes one's body language.

Learning Points :

* Body also speaks.

* Our every action and each posture convey messages.

* Interpretations of one's body language by another person depends on her/his perceptions, which are based on her/his beliefs.

* One must dare to dream fantastic dreams about ones life. One should not feel guilty about dreaming good things for one self. In order to achieve higher goals in one's life first of all one must dream them. If you get scared even to dream good things for yourself then how can you have good things for yourself.

* During interaction one should not only listen to the cells of ones body but also listen to the body language of others in order to get maximum out of the communication.

Exercise on "Crystal River and Creatures"

A fantasy exercise on "Crystal River and creatures" helped the participants to get in touch with their inner self and relate to similar situations in one's life. It gave an insight to the following :

* It is easy to cling on to something and feel good or had about it.

* When we cling to something (something refers to persons, things and, situations) then it persists to exist in our life. It becomes part of our existence and dictates life for us. We also then start taking it for granted that it should be so. It then blocks our growth because we then incapacitate self from seeing beyond. If you want to get in touch with your creative self then you must learn to see beyond. Do not block your vision. If you block your vision then you can not move forward. So identify what factors are blocking your vision, in other words what factors are blocking your growth. You get the clues by discovering to what are you clinging.

* Learn to let go and float. When you do this your vision gets cleared.

* While letting go do not struggle because if you struggle then whatever you are trying to let go sticks to you. When you want to let go something just drop it. Let it exist independent of you. Then you become free from it. It can not dictate terms to you. Now you not only can see beyond but also have a new way of relating to it.

* There is always a way to achieve something and it depends upon the choices made by self.

* I can be my own savior. I also can be my own path.

* When you want to achieve something in your life first of all you must trust self. The word 'risk' was replaced by 'trust.'

* Keeping dumb and inert serve no purpose at all. Participate in life fully in order to have fuller life.

Participants were also challenged concretely to let go :

> oppressive beliefs,
> oppressive relationships,
> oppressive images of persons,
> things that made one feel secure,
> situations that kept on repeating.

Clinging is like addiction, when you let go you get new energy and more time and energy are available to you to be creative.

'Who Am I ?' :

The session was ment to create awareness of "Self", "Who am I ?", "My feeling" and "My behaviour" in various situations and with various people.

To begin with, the participants were asked to form 2 concentric circles, one facing the other and made to rotate one in clockwise direction and the other in anticlock wise direction. While moving in a circle, the participants were asked to look at the (i) eyes of the partner (ii) partner's palms (iii) feet of the partner (iv) whole body of the partner, all the while concentrating on WHO ARE YOU ?

Later experiences and feelings shared by the participants were,

Inability to concentrate on "Who are you ?"

Peace and happiness.

Thought of different persons.

Fear to look at other's eyes.

Comfortable.

Uncomfortable.

Looking at Oneself in the Mirror :

Every human being wears different masks for different times and situations and tries to project a different "himself" or "herself". He feels comfortable wearing various masks.

"Who am I ?" To discover this, one should remove all the masks worn and face one's real life.

This fact was arrived at through a fantasy exercise.

Later the participants were given the following questions.

1. What did you feel last after removing the masks ?

2. Why do you wear masks when you interact with people ?

3. What kind of masks do you wear in your day to day life ?

Feelings After Removing the Masks :

* Fear
* Restlessness
* Calm
* Peaceful
* Powerlessness
* Happiness

Why we wear Masks :

* To hide our real life.
* To make people happy.
* To face a situation.
* To hide our weakness.
* To be accepted and wanted.
* Because we do not accept ourselves.
* Because of fear and insecurity.

Different Kinds of Masks Worn :

* Faithfulness	(Dog)
* Cunning	(Cat)
* Proud and happiness	(Peacock)
* Strong and mighty	(Elephant)
* Escapism	(Rabbit)
* Power/Authority	(Tiger)
* Purity and peace	(Dove)

Deepening the Awareness of One's Own Body :

Participants did an exercise to become aware of thoughts and feelings as well as their body.

Trainer pointed out that each one should be aware of what his/her body tells to him/her. One should listen to one's body. Self knowledge and awareness is very important to plan and perform better. More we are aware of our body, thoughts and feelings, the more energy we get. We get energy through thoughts, feelings and behaviours. Behaviour differs from one person to another because each ones thoughts differ. When you change your thoughts you become a different person. By changing the pattern of your thoughts you can organise and reorganise your energy.

Past has gone and future is uncertain. Only the present is here. Eternity is now. Live fully in this moment of 'Now'. Living fully in the eternal now opens a door way for you to know yourself. It helps to transcend the ego. When you become aware of yourself, you will get in touch with your potentials, more energy will be available to you and your confidence will increase.

All human beings have self worth because of eternally who we are. When you cannot control your thoughts and judgments, do not struggle with it. Only be in touch with the present and experience the magic of more energy being available to you. The more aware we are, the more choices we have. We are free to make different choices, as the situation changes. But when we are aware of the choices made we do not take the consequences as sufferings, pains, but as challenges and opportunities.

Exercise to Make Oneself Aware of the Body :

The participants were asked to keep their eyes closed, take deep breath, be aware of the sensations. They were asked to focus on any one part of the body for a prolonged period of time and feel the sensations. Later it was shared in the group.

It is amazing to get in touch with various sensations, after a certain period of time (it may take different amount of time for different people) you can feel the energy flow in that body part.

Profile of Myself :

Each one was asked to draw the profile of himself/herself. This helped the participants to assess themselves, how far, one knows about already concretised strengths of self.

Dialogue with My Work :

It is essential to know that only mechanically doing work blocks the energy of self and the quality of work gets reduced. The following exercise was done to be aware of ones relationship to work and to deepen the relationship.

The participants were asked to personify their work and give life to it and have a dialogue with it. This was an amazing and enthralling experience to the participants and it made the participants to go deeper and deeper to oneself with respect what work really means to the person and to assess the personal factors that create bottle necks and prevent the person from giving expected output and reduce the efficiency and effectivity. This added another dimension to expand ones awareness about self. Dialogue process helped the participants to understand one's feelings at different situations, attitudes and how to be more creative at work.

Questions for Reflection :

* What kind of change do you like to bring in your work ?

* What would you do to make your work enjoyable ?

* What core beliefs do you have about your work ?

* What is your attitude towards the work you do ?

Sharing :

I feel bored with my job.

I have to work so I work.

Ultimately I have to do so to earn my living so I do.

So much to do and no one to help, I am tired of it.

It is my duty so I do it sometimes I have to force myself.

Learning points :

Add life to your work.

* Be more innovative and creative.

* Enjoy what you do.

* Beliefs about the work need to be changed. Beliefs make all the difference because beliefs are alive and active.

* Attitude towards work is manifested through the quality of our work.

* The every process of working builds self and helps a person to grow.

* The work that we do represents us, hence it is important to be disciplined about the quality the work we do.

* Let your work be a creation.

* One has to be serious about the quality of work however small or big the work is.

* Enjoy the whole process of work, let the joy flow through out and not only as an outcome of accomplishment.

Seeing Through the Illusion :

Participants were facilitated to enter into a meditative mood.

Absolute silence was maintained.

Each participant was asked to hold a dry twig in hand and give focused attention to the twig.

After some time the participants were asked to love the twig by giving loving attention to it.

Later some of the participant shared their experiences.

The dryness of the twig was an allusion. The twig was full of energy. Each part of the twig is full of energy so as rest of the creation.

Keep on giving loving attention to it.

Drive home points were :

* Every creation of God has its own beauty and life.

* Every creation has its own " SELF WORTH".

* One should be able to identify this "WORTH" of others and respect.

* Accept people as they are and for what they are.

* Appreciate things as they are.

* If you can love a dry twig you can love anything and anyone.

* The actual beneficiary is the lover and not the loved object.

* You can increase your energy by being in love.

* Loving need not be spontaneous. An intention, a decision is suffice.

* Love creates more love.

Recalling One's Past Life :

Session was on recalling one's past life, noting down some incidents, sharing with other and assessing what was learnt by this exercise.

Participants were asked to write down the important events in their life, both pleasant and unpleasant and to choose three they considered as most important ones.

Later the participants were made to get in touch with their inner sensations and to come back slowly to their present life.

Recalling the incidents helped them to make important decisions and take their own unique paths. Noting down the decisions and paths taken and not taken helped the participants to discover what they considered consciously or unconsciously as priority areas in their life.

Decisions not made are also decisions. The paths that are not taken might still be opportunities and aspects of self that might need growth. Exploring and being aware of these potential areas within self helps the person to achieve balance. This process also helps the person to concretise one's potential.

Learning Points of the Whole Training :
1. Every one is the creator of his/her own realities.
2. Every one is the range of possibilities.
3. One should be aware of oneself to enjoy the "REAL SELF"
4. Eternity is now and present actions have a cumulative effect.
5. Every incident in one's life need not determine one's life.
6. Every one has the right to make his/her own choices.
7. Every one is responsible for his/her happiness and sufferings.
8. One should be aware of the masks he/she wears in the day to day life.
9. Each one is unique and has his/her own intrinsic worth.
10. More we are aware of our body, thoughts and feelings, more energy we receive.
11. There is a lot beyond the physical "me" and there are no boundaries or parameters beyond which the mind cannot travel.

Outcome of the Training as Expressed by the Participants :

Training helped
* To identify and discharge one's feelings.
* To discharge one's blocked energies.

* To think about oneself more critically and consciously.
* To feel energised.
* To rejuvenate one's energy.
* To reflect and find out the "REAL ME" in me.
* To open up new avenues of thinking.
* To change the outlook of life and have alternative perspective of life that helps to get fulfilled in life.
* To move closer to one's being and not to be driven away by the indulgence of the ego in myths and illusions.

HUMAN PROCESS LAB : 3
BEING SELF RESOURCEFUL

Objectives :

To increase participants awareness of Self

To enable the participants to gain clarity on the core principles of the present perspective of living.

To develop harmonious inter personal relationships.

To enable the participants to realise their potentialities.

Day I : The training started at 10.00 a.m. with the relaxation exercise. While doing the relaxation exercise the participants were helped to have two questions at the back of their mind : "Who are you ?" "Why are you here ?"

During the sharing, the participants expressed the following answers.

* I am MYSELF. I am here to undergo training.
* I am a human being. I am here to learn about self.
* I am a loving creation of God and full of energy. I am born in this world with a purpose.

Resource person facilitated a process for the participants to have a profound reflection on Who am I ? and Why am I here ?

Participants were then guided to have a walk in silence on hill side with mindfulness. The landscape provided the environment required for the walk. The participants were asked to be friendly with their inner self and as they walked to reflect about their relationship with earth.

What kind of energy do I receive from earth ?

What do I give back ?

What is my attitude towards this mother earth ? Is it a nurturing relationship or only using and exploitative ?

Do I own this earth ? or am I a part of it ?

Almost all the participants enjoyed the walk though it was a difficult walk since the landscape was stony and covered with thorny bushes. In fact for many of the participants it was first time walking uphill in the sun.

For most of the participants it was a deep experience, they received a lot of energy from the 'earth' and found it quite refreshing. They had forgotten all about stress in their life. It opened up a new dimension of relating to nature and receiving strength from it. They also developed a special nurturing bond with 'earth'.

Change Can Come Immediately : Mountain Climbing

In the hot sun of middle noon the participants were challenged to climb a mountain. Some of the participants thought they could enjoy climbing a mountain only either in the morning or in the evening. Others thought they could never climb a mountain. Some thought they would even become sick if they climb a mountain. Ultimately the entire team decided to climb the beautiful mountain. Though there was a hesitation among the few participants in the beginning, they were motivated to take it as a challenge and then it was possible for the team to make a quick decision. Each one took it as a challenge.

After climbing, almost all the participants were surprised that they had not only climbed a mountain in the hot sun, but also enjoyed climbing.

The process of climbing the mountain helped the participants to let go some of the preconceived notions and beliefs. There was a reflection on how we get conditioned and limit ourselves from aspiring for higher goals.

Some of the participants felt rejuvenated with energy-both physical and mental.

Some of the other insights gained by the participants are as follows :

* There is no good time or bad time to do a task, what we require is a firm intention, a decision to do the task then we can shackle all barriers and pre conditions.

* An invididual can get motivated by the energy of the team.

* We experience limitations due to our conditioned state. It is possible to decondition self and go for what we want.

* When we free ourselves from the preconditioned state we can achieve something extraordinary.

* Inner change can occur immediately. It need not be a long process. What requires is drop and let go the limiting belief.

* Our thoughts, *i.e.*, our beliefs make us who we are.

Yoga : The resource person taught certain yoga exercises to the participants.

DAY II : Relaxation of Body and Mind — To relax each and every muscle of the body and the mind, the participants were asked to do body movements.

As a second part of the exercise the participants were asked to listen to their internal state and make appropriate sound that the body asked for. This session lasted for nearly 40 minutes.

During the next session the participants danced to the tune of a music. This was a session on learning to discover the rhythm of the body.

Participants found the session helpful to gain more insights into the body and self.

Meditation : In order to be at ease and peace both physically and mentally, the resource person facilitated and put the participants into a deep meditative state.

Meditation helps the individual to glide within self and know more about self. It also helps a person to go deeper and deeper into oneself and have a inner vision of self. It also helps an individual to concentrate on one thing which enhances the flow of inner energy which can ultimately result in both effective and result oriented performances and also realise oneself if one wants to.

The participants experienced healing energy within onself and amidst the group. After the sharing from the participants of all the three exercises it was time for lunch.

If We Think That We Can, We Can :

The participants were challenged to do something which they never did before and to accomplish the task within the stipulated time.

'IF WE THINK THAT WE CAN, WE CAN.' This was proved by the team by taking the work of manufacturing 100 bricks within the stipulated time. Before starting, the team worked out the possibilities and thought of the resources available. The participants also went through a process of feeling uncertain about being able to do the task and also accomplishing it within the stipulated time.

This was a thrilling experience to all the participants and a moment of joy when the team was able to finish making 100 bricks as promised. Participants were shocked about their own capacities. The fulfillment of the target gave the team a sense of satisfaction and pleasure. Team spirit was there through out the work.

DAY III : The day's session was started with a change. The team was moved to an isolated place amidst the forest where there was a stream of water and shelter.

Each one was asked to be still with nature, feel it and to get energy from the natural surroundings. Think discreetly about "Who Am I ?" And draw a picture depicting oneself.

Later sharing from each participant.

Some of them are : Sun, Candle, Bird, Star, Coconut tree, A source of energy, Stream of water, Part of nature.

During the post lunch session the participants were asked to reflect on the following :

* Who do you think who you are ?

* What does the society think about who you are ?

* What are the conflict areas ?

Sharing from the participants. Some of the identified conflict areas are :

* I am sincere but others think that I am selfish.

* I am a small creature on this earth but the society thinks that I am the saviour.

* I am not confident of doing things. But others think that I am an achiever.

  I am powerless. But others think that I am powerful.

* I cannot say no to people and I always think that others are right and I am wrong.

* I can not assert myself.

The sharing was continued for the next day also.

DAY IV : Sharing regarding the conflict areas was continued in the morning session.

After the tea break, the resource person asked the participants to write a **Legend on 'Myself'.**

Sharing from the team.

On each and every sharing from the participant, the faculty used to reflect on it and give inputs.

Post lunch session was meant for physical work. The participants worked in the field. The day was ended with meditation.

DAY V : Day started with silence and reflection on the previous day's session.

The participants were asked to look at their left palm and concentrate fully.

And after some time to hold the right foot in the left hand and concentrate.

Then each one shared his/her experiences.

The learning point of this exercise was that each part of the body is important and it emits energy because it is energy. Some participants were very sensitive to energy. The exercise also helped to focus and after some prolonged period to transcend the ego.

The collective energy can do wonders.

Learning Points :

1. Human beings are neither powerful nor powerless. We just are.
2. Power is for growth.
3. All human beings are cocreators with God.
4. Every one can create his or her own reality.
5. Now is eternal. Past and future do not exist, they are only illusions.

6. Every one is full of inner strength and energy. In order to have this inner energy you only need to be aware of it.

7. Unconditional Love frees you from controlling relationships.

8. Every human being is a combination of body, mind and spirit. To keep them in a harmonious state is the responsibility of the human beings.

9. The secret of quality energy is to love others unconditionally. Quality energy can come from within.

10. It is very important to be honest to oneself.

11. Change can take place immediately. That is you who can bring change.

12. It is a liberating experience to be free from all preconditions.

13. Thoughts are our stream of consciousness. Be aware of your thoughts.

14. Every part of the human being has energy points.

15. It is essential to be peaceful and restful.

16. We can break all the barriers at any point of time and can do wonders.

17. Awareness is healing.

    Paying attention is healing.

    Trusting is healing.

    Energy is healing.

18. Be still and know that you are.

19. One can transfer healing energy to others.

20. Expansion of energy leads to healing and happiness.

21. Our energy gets organised (disorganised) depending on the conditioning of our mind. When we get deconditioned we can create new patterns of our energy.

22. The set patterns decide our personality.

23. Flow of energy comes from within.

24. We have different keys within us. We have to identify and unlock the blocks.

25. Life is a range of possibilities. Every one has his/her choices.

Participant's Opinion about the Programme :

The programme helped me to :

Go deeper into myself to understand myself better.

Understand that I am a life giver.

Strengthen the relationship between me and nature.

Keep my energy level high by learning tension releasing techniques. —*Jessi Britto.*

Break self made barrers and to live the moment.

Reflect on my own beliefs and change them.

Know changes are immediate.

Relate to nature and draw energy from nature and to be full of energy.

Know the utilisation of energy and purification of body and revitalising it.

Embrace and love me, others and nature.—*Victor Tauro*

Be more aware of myself, thoughts and actions and inner strength.

Love myself and others and nature.

Learn to change the beliefs and to take challenges.

Experience giving and receiving energy. —*Stella Kumari*

Feel the energy and pleasure within myself.

Increase the inner healing energy and to channelise the same.

Love myself, my work and to keep the energy level high.

Be genuine towards my feelings and body needs.

Change my beliefs and be aware of my thoughts.

Take challenges in my life.

Realise that I am the saviour of myself.

—*Walter D'Souza.*

Gain strength, be aware of myself, my thoughts and each part of my body.

Realise that I should love my body and it is full of energy.

Be calm and ease after meditation and mass.

Forget the past and concentrate on the present.

—*Mohini Poojari*

Bibliography

1. Adler, A. The Practice and Theory of Individual Psychology. New York, IIarcourt, Brace & World, 1927.
   "A Theory of Therapy, Personality and Interpersonal Relationships, as developed in the Client-Centered Framework", in Sigmund Koch (ed.), Psychology : A Study of a Science, Volume III, N. Y., McGraw-Hill, 1969, p. 234-235.

2. Bandler, Richard and Grinder, John, (1975) The Structure of Magic I, Science and Behaviour Books, INc., Palo Alto, Ca.,

3. Bandler, Richard and Grinder, John, (1976). The Structure of Magic II, Science and Behaviour Books, Inc., Palo Alto, Ca.,

4. Benson (1976). The Relaxation Response. William Morrow, New York.

5. Claudio Naranjo and Robert Ornstein, (1971), On the Psychology of Meditation, New York.

6. Davis 1994 A Master Guide to Meditation & Spiritual Growth. 22-24-25-27, 34-37, CSA Press Publishers, Lakemont, Georgia 30552.

7. Erikson E. 11 Childhood & Society. New York, Norton Sec. Edition Revised 1963.

8. Erikson, E. II., Identity : Youth and Crisis, New York, Norton, 1968.

9. Freud, S., (1964) An Outline of Psycho-analysis. In Standard Edition, Vol. 23. London, Hogarth Press.

10. Fromm, E. (1941) Escape from Freedom, New York, Rinehart.

11. Geetz, C. 1958. Ethos, World-View and the Analysis of Sacred Symbols. Antioch Review, Winter (1957-8).

12. Goodenough, Ward II. 1957, "Cultural Anthropology and Linguistics." In Paul Garvin (ed), Report of the Seventh Annual Round Table Meeting on Linguistics and Language Study, Georgetown Monograph Series, 9, Washington, D.C. Georgetown University Press.

13. Hewitt (1992), Teach Yourself Meditation. NTC Publishing Group, 4255 West Touhy Avenue, Loncwood, Illinois, 60646-U.S.A.

14. Jung, C.G., 1952, "Psychology and Literature," In Brewster Ghiselin, (ed.), The Creative Process, New York.

15. Jung, C. G., Collected Works. H. Read, M. Fordham, and g. Adler (Eds.). Princeton, Princeton Univ. Press, 1953-1978.

16. Jung, C. G., The Structure and Dynamics of the Psyche. In Collected Works. Vol. 8, Princeton, Princeton Univ. Press, 1960.

17. Krishnamurti, J., (1975), Beginnings of Learning, Penguin Books, Ltd., Harmondsworth, Middlesex, England.

18. Levy, Monto "The Medicine Within,"

19. Maslow (1962), Towards A Psychology of Being.

Van Nostrand, Princeton, N. J.

20. Maslow (1970), Motivation and Personality, N. Y., Harper and Row.

21. Maslow (1974), "Personality Problems and Personaliy Growth," in Clark E. Moustakas (ed.),

22. The Self-Explorations in Personal Growth, N.Y., Harper Colophon Books, P. 232-233.

23. Masters (1989), "Self-Hypnosis and its Relation to Metaphysical Practice."

24. Masters Degree Level Lesson, university of Metaphysics, California.

25. Mookerjee (1995), Kundalini The Arousal of the Inner Energy Thames and Hudson Ltd, London.

26. Rama (1988), Path of Fire Light. Volume II.
The Himalayan International Institute of Yoga Science and Philosophy of the U.S.A.

27. Honesdale, Pennsylvania 18431.

28. Sullivan, II. S., (1953), The Interpersonal Theory of Psychiatry, N.Y., W. W. Norton.

29. Unknown Author, The Cloud of Unknowing, William Johnston (Ed. 1973), Image Books, A Division of Doubleday & Co., Garden City, New York.